NYLON

UNIVERSE

UNIVERSE

NYLON

PLAY

THE NYLON BOOK OF MUSIC

Music has always been an extremely important part of my life, as it is for many people. So of course, when I started NYLON, I knew music would be as much a part of the magazine as fashion and beauty—just channeled through the brand's defining edgy aesthetic.

I love girl bands and female vocalists, and it's always been interesting to find and meet new bands who I think fit with the NYLON sensibility. As you can see by the artists in this book, we pay homage to the icons of the '60s, '70s, '80s, and '90s, just as much as we try to be on point when it comes to the latest bands. I encourage everyone in the office to talk about their band obsessions, so we're always introducing each other to cool new sounds, and that enthusiasm for music affects the entire magazine—from someone finding out about a new band from an intern and then doing a feature on it to the way we present our fashion and beauty coverage.

Since NYLON launched nearly nine years ago, the way that people listen to music has changed a lot. Of course, there's the advent of iTunes, which has let people share music more easily, but the mixing of music and computers has also made the entire scene more global. London, for example, has always played an important part in everything creative that I do, and I still always get inspired by music that comes from there, but now I think everyone's scope is broadening. These days, we're as likely to write about bands from Paris (like the Plastiscines) or Brazil (like CSS) as we are bands from New York and L.A.—and again, I think this book reflects that.

Music is so much a part of the DNA of the magazine that it was only logical that the third NYLON book (following STREET: The NYLON Book of Global Style and PRETTY: The NYLON Book of Beauty) should be devoted to it. PLAY is about getting inspired—whether it's by dressing like Chrissie Hynde, or making MixTapes, or checking out the songs that Eisley or the MisShapes recommend. So go ahead, press play.

Marvin Scott-Jarrett, editor-in-chief, NYLON

**DO YOU REMEMBER LYING IN BED /
WITH THE COVERS PULLED UP OVER YOUR HEAD /
RADIO PLAYIN' SO NO ONE CAN SEE?
"DO YOU REMEMBER ROCK 'N' ROLL RADIO?"
— THE RAMONES**

I do.

In fourth grade I had a little red transistor radio from RadioShack that I would sneak into bed with me after I was told it was time to turn my lights out and go to sleep. Buried underneath the blankets, the tiny radio pressed to my ear, I'd listen to Casey Kasem counting down the Top 40, the sound lowered to a static-blurred whisper. A few years later, when my taste began to mature out of the mainstream and into the more obscure, I'd sneak into the living room and watch *120 Minutes* on MTV, which introduced me to bands I love to this day (the Smiths, the Cure, the Pixies) and completely blew my middle-of-nowhere, middle American mind. Sometimes I'd even tape the show on a crummy cassette recorder, since in those pre-Internet times there was no other way for me to hear those songs again—and I still have those tapes in a box in my closet, even though they're now too warped to play.

In one way or another, music has always been an important part of my life. One of my very first memories is of lying on my stomach next to my mother on our shag-pile living-room carpet (avocado green—it was the '70s), with the Beatles' *Sgt. Pepper's Lonely Hearts Club Band* album sleeve laid out on the floor in front of us. We were playing a game. My mother would tap the faces of the four mustachioed men smiling up at us from the gatefold, from right to left, and I would try to name them: George, Paul, John…the last one was always easiest because it reminded me of a song I sang in school—"Ringo was his name-o."

I vividly remember too the first album I ever owned that was mine, not my older sister's or my parents'. It was a K-Tel compilation called *Rock 80*, and I got it for Christmas the same glorious year that I got a pair of roller skates. Much to my mother's chagrin, I would play that album over and over again at top volume while skating around the house (the aforementioned green carpet, thankfully, was long gone). I can still name every track—Gary Numan's "Cars," Pat Benatar's "Heartbreaker," Joe Jackson's "Is She Really Going Out With Him?", Blondie's "Call Me," The Knack's "My Sharona," Cheap Trick's "I Want You To Want Me" among them. In a lot of ways, those songs still inform my musical taste today. The first track on side two, incidentally, was "Do You Remember Rock 'n' Roll Radio?" by the Ramones.

There may be people who have no favorite book or TV show or movie or magazine (although, hello, *NYLON*!), but there's no one who doesn't have a favorite song. They can no doubt remember when they first heard it or tell you (at length) why it's so meaningful to them, even if it's as simple as the fact that it always makes them want to get up and dance. Music is something that shapes who you are. It touches other areas of your life, as well—how you dress, whom you relate to, what you respond to in art or films or car commercials. And when you hear something that moves you, or removes you from your present circumstance—those riveting, transcendent moments at concerts; a cheesy lite-FM song piped into the grocery store that suddenly *speaks* to you—the experience can even be life-changing. Such moments are rare and golden and beautiful, and they are exactly why cavemen started beating out rhythms with buffalo bones around a campfire.

I wanted *PLAY* to be all about inspiration, because really, that's what music itself is all about. While putting it together, I replayed the records that have meant the most to me, and talked to a lot of people about their favorites—which in turn introduced me to exciting new songs and albums that I had never heard before. I chose to focus primarily on women, not because I'm trying to make a point (although the world would definitely be a better place if more girls picked up guitars) but because I needed to narrow it down—and *NYLON* is, after all, geared toward the ladies. In fact, one of the many things that makes working at *NYLON* such a pleasure and a thrill for me is that it recognizes that girls love music just as much as anyone else. Music magazines are male-biased, but loving music isn't. It's universal. There's a magic to it that's perhaps too precious and elusive to try and deconstruct here or anywhere else, but personally, I have learned this: Playing music (whether it's on a guitar, a turntable, or an iPod) is as essential to life as, well, playing. And I sincerely hope that *PLAY* inspires you to do all of the above.

— April Long, executive editor, *NYLON*

IN EVERY GENERATION AND IN EVERY GENRE, THERE HAVE BEEN MUSICIANS WHO STAND APART AS BEING INNOVATORS; WHO ARE (OR HAVE BEEN) TRULY CREATIVE, UNIQUE, AND INSPIRING. THEY ARE ICONIC BECAUSE SOMETHING ABOUT THEM—BE IT THEIR EYE-CATCHING PERSONAL STYLE, THEIR REBELLIOUS ROCK 'N' ROLL ATTITUDE, OR SONGS THEY'VE PENNED THAT STAND THE TEST OF TIME—HAS STRUCK A CHORD WITH MUSIC-LOVERS AND INCITED OTHERS TO FOLLOW THE PATHS THEY'VE BLAZED. THE LADIES WE'VE CHOSEN TO CELEBRATE ON THE FOLLOWING PAGES DIDN'T JUST EARN THEIR ICON STATUS THROUGH FAME OR RECORD SALES, BUT BECAUSE THEY'RE THE ARTISTS WHO KEEP MUSIC MOVING FORWARD, AND WHO KEEP US ALWAYS WANTING TO HEAR MORE.

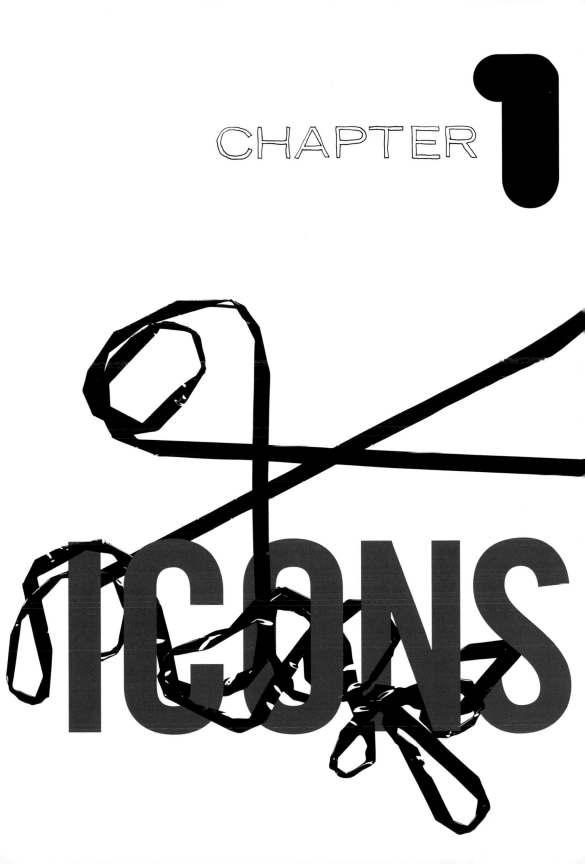

CHAPTER **1**

ICONS

MARIANNE FAITHFULL

I AM A MUSE NOT A MISTRESS, NOT A WHORE
— "SLIDING THROUGH LIFE ON CHARM"

Born in 1946 to a college professor and a Viennese baroness—her great-uncle was Austro-Hungarian nobleman Leopold von Sacher-Masoch, whose nineteenth-century novel *Venus in Furs* introduced the word *masochism*, and later provided the Velvet Underground with a song title—Marianne Faithfull was discovered by Rolling Stones manager Andrew Loog Oldham at a party. Enchanted by the seventeen-year-old's beauty, he instructed Mick Jagger and Keith Richards to write a song for her, and the result, "As Tears Go By," became her first hit single (she later repaid the favor by co-writing "Sister Morphine" with them). In the beginning she looked like a prim schoolgirl—all Peter Pan collars, Mary Janes, and an innocent stare—but that didn't last long once she became romantically involved with Jagger. As the couple who most epitomized Swinging London, there were sex and drug scandals aplenty—she was famously branded "the girl in the fur rug" by the British press after a police raid on Richards's country home found her wearing nothing else. Faithfull eventually gave in to her heroin addiction, living penniless on the streets for nearly two years, before making a major comeback in 1979 with the raw-nerved album *Broken English*, in which the shy, soft singing voice of her early years was supplanted by a gravelly, world-weary squawk. In her music as in her life, Faithfull has always favored experimentation over conformity and has collaborated with artists as diverse as David Bowie, Beck, Tom Waits, PJ Harvey, Metallica, Nick Cave, and Jarvis Cocker (check out her 2002 album, *Kissin' Time*, on which many of these artists appear), and her nonchalant, salty-survivor brand of cool has inspired everyone from Courtney Love to Kate Moss.

HEAR

Marianne Faithfull (1965)
Marianne's first U.S. release includes "As Tears Go By," "This Little Bird" (the lyrics are inspired by Tennessee Williams's *Orpheus Descending*) and, oddly, covers of both "Greensleeves" and "House of the Rising Sun."

READ

Faithfull: An Autobiography (1994)
Faithfull has said "I have lived my life as an adventure, and I wouldn't change much about it." In her riveting first autobiography (a second was published in 2007), she unrepentantly recounts it all—from giving Jagger sweet satisfaction as a naive (but, incidentally, married) teenager to her extended stay in junkieville to her arduous recovery.

WATCH

Girl on a Motorcycle (1968)
In which Faithfull gets kitted out in head-to-toe leather, embarks on a psychedelic road trip across Europe, and has steamy trysts with suave Eurohunk Alain Delon (it earned an X rating upon its stateside release, with the much more titillating title *Naked Under Leather*).

WEAR

Trenchcoat
Channel Faithfull's demure-with-a-menswear-twist look in a classic trench and retro scarf. Then go out and find yourself some trouble.

PRIMP

Pale pink lipstick
She didn't need to compete with Mick's pout.

The Velvet Underground and Nico (1967)
With its strange, experimental sound-scapes, proto-punk ennui, and garage rock rattle and hum, this is, quite simply, one of the most influential records of all time.

Chelsea Girl (1967)
Nico's monotone Teutonic drone has a tendency to polar-ize listeners, but her string-laden debut solo album, with songs written by Jackson Browne and Bob Dylan, is truly as bleakly beautiful as it is off-puttingly odd.

READ

NICO

SONGS THEY
NEVER PLAY
ON THE
RADIO

JAMES YOUNG

Songs They Never Play On The Radio
James Young
Written by a member of Nico's tour-ing band late in her career—when, addicted to heroin, she was performing freaky, funereal gigs in dingy clubs across Europe—this account is sad (and sadly out-of-print), harrowing, surpris-ingly hilarious, and well-worth tracking down.

HERE SHE COMES, YOU'D
BETTER WATCH YOUR STEP /
SHE'S GOING TO BREAK YOUR
HEART IN TWO, IT'S TRUE
— "FEMME FATALE"

NICO

Model, actress, and singer Nico lived a life stranger than fiction, bouncing from continent to continent and in and out of the beds of some of the most wanted men in showbiz (Jim Morrison, Bob Dylan, Lou Reed, John Cale, Iggy Pop, and Brian Jones were all on her conquest list, along with actor Alain Delon, with whom she had a son). Born Christa Päffgen in Nazi-controlled Germany in 1938, she took up modeling in Berlin following her father's death in a concentration camp. Nicknamed "Nico" by a photographer friend, she was spotted by Federico Fellini while in Rome and cast in *La Dolce Vita*. In the early '60s, she attended acting classes with Marilyn Monroe and in 1964, she released her first single, a cover of the Gordon Lightfoot song "I'm Not Sayin,'" produced by Jimmy Page on Rolling Stones manager Andrew Loog Oldham's label. Dylan introduced her to Andy Warhol and she began starring in his experimental films, which led to her induction into the Velvet Underground, at that time essentially the Factory house band. In 1967 her icy, dispassionate vocals graced three tracks on their classic debut, *The Velvet Underground and Nico*, but the German chanteuse was booted from the band afterward due to tension between her and Reed. She went on to write and perform, often with Cale, some of the most provocative and chilling music of the '60s and '70s until her death on July 18, 1988, from a stroke she suffered while riding her bike in Ibiza.

DOWNLOAD "These Days"

MOE TUCKER

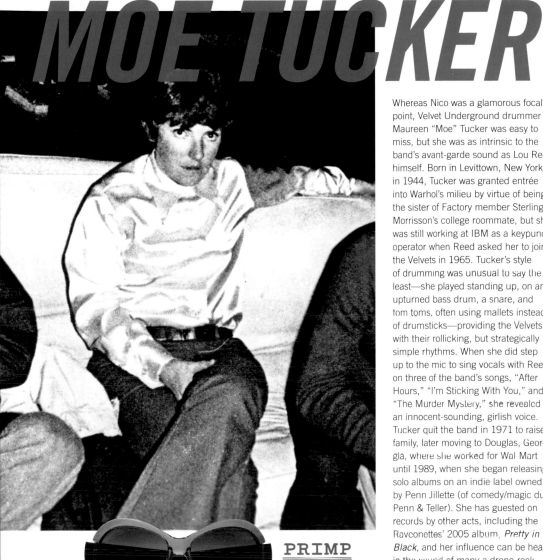

Whereas Nico was a glamorous focal point, Velvet Underground drummer Maureen "Moe" Tucker was easy to miss, but she was as intrinsic to the band's avant-garde sound as Lou Reed himself. Born in Levittown, New York, in 1944, Tucker was granted entrée into Warhol's milieu by virtue of being the sister of Factory member Sterling Morrisson's college roommate, but she was still working at IBM as a keypunch operator when Reed asked her to join the Velvets in 1965. Tucker's style of drumming was unusual to say the least—she played standing up, on an upturned bass drum, a snare, and tom toms, often using mallets instead of drumsticks—providing the Velvets with their rollicking, but strategically simple rhythms. When she did step up to the mic to sing vocals with Reed on three of the band's songs, "After Hours," "I'm Sticking With You," and "The Murder Mystery," she revealed an innocent-sounding, girlish voice. Tucker quit the band in 1971 to raise a family, later moving to Douglas, Georgia, where she worked for Wal-Mart until 1989, when she began releasing solo albums on an indie label owned by Penn Jillette (of comedy/magic duo Penn & Teller). She has guested on records by other acts, including the Raveonettes' 2005 album, *Pretty in Black*, and her influence can be heard in the sound of many a drone-rock band, perhaps most significantly, the Jesus and Mary Chain, who wrote a song about her in 1998.

PRIMP

Black sunglasses
Moe wore her
sunglasses
at night.

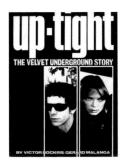

READ

***Up-Tight: the Velvet
Underground Story***
**Victor Bockris and
Gerard Malaga**
Where to get
your Moe down.

HEAR

The Velvet Underground
(1969)
Moe's vocals on
"After Hours," plus
the mournful "Candy
Says" and the linger-
ing-on-love song
"Pale Blue Eyes"
equal the Velvet's
prettiest album.

DOWNLOAD "I'm Sticking with You"

SO WON'T YOU A SAY YOU LOVE ME / I'LL MAKE YOU
SO PROUD OF ME WE'LL MAKE THEM TURN THEIR HEADS
EVERY PLACE WE GO — "BE MY BABY"

RONNIE SPECTOR

HEAR

*The Best of The
Ronettes* (1992)
Ronnie's voice
defined an
entire era.
This is why.

READ

*Be My Baby: How I
Survived Mascara,
Miniskirts, and
Madness*
**Ronnie Spector with
Vince Waldron**
Now out of
print, Ronnie's
autobiography
goes for big
bucks, but
it's worth
seeking out.

With her bouffant black beehive, bodacious body, and lashings of black eyeliner, Ronnie Bennett was a serious babe—it's no wonder the craziest man in rock 'n' roll (that would be Phil) scooped her up and married her. The Ronettes, initially called The Darling Sisters (Ronnie, her sister Estelle, and their cousin Nedra Talley), began performing at New York's famed Peppermint Lounge in 1961 when they were in their early teens. By 1963 they had recorded their first Number 1 single, the now-classic "Be My Baby," with Phil Spector's signature Wall of Sound production technique setting them leagues apart from any other girl group on the scene. Ronnie's unmistakable delivery—a mixture of vulnerability and street-wise toughness—gave the group an added dimension, and some of their many time-less songs, like "Walking in the Rain," were tinged with an almost sinister darkness. After she wed Phil in 1968, he kept her virtually imprisoned in their home, releasing only her 1971 single (written and produced by George Harrison), "Try Some Buy Some." But tough chick that she is, Ronnie eventually broke away and went on to achieve solo stardom—no-tably with a 1986 Number 1 duet with Eddie Money, "Take Me Home Tonight"; and an excellent 1999 EP on indie label Kill Rock Stars, which was produced by longtime fan Joey Ramone and included "Don't Worry Baby," which Beach Boy Brian Wilson had written especially for her. In 2006, she released her first full-length album in thirty years, *The Last of the Rock Stars.*

PRIMP

Black mascara
Lay it on
thick, baby.

Hair extensions
What, you thought that
was her real hair?

FRANÇOISE HARDY

HEAR

Comment Te Dire Adieu (1968)
The album which per-
haps best encompasses
Hardy's range—from the
charming, playful pop
of the title track to
her mournfully chill-
ing cover of Leonard
Cohen's "Suzanne" (en
Français, bien sûr!).

A French beauty *nonpareil*, Françoise
Hardy rose to fame as part of the '60s Yé-yé
scene (a Gallic teen-pop phenomenon)
with her 1965 hit song, "Tout les Garçons
et les Filles," which sold two million copies
in eighteen months. A tall, thin, shy girl
with a delightfully soft voice, Hardy had
studied politics and literature before signing
a recording contract at the age of seventeen
(unlike most *chanteuses* of the time, she
wrote nearly all of her own songs). The
antithesis of a giddy girl star, Hardy had an
elegant, tranquil quality, and despite her
striking beauty, she was never marketed for
her sex appeal. In 1966, she appeared in
Jean-Luc Godard's Nouvelle Vague masterpiece *Masculin, Féminin*, and released her
first English album, which enchanted Britain
and America with its nostalgic, romantic
lyrics. Her international renown was such
that she hung out with the Beatles, Bob
Dylan (who invited her up to his hotel room
after a concert but failed to seduce her),
and Mick Jagger, who once called her his
"ideal woman." She quit touring in 1968
and vowed that she would stop singing
before she turned fifty—then recorded her
"farewell" album, *Decalage*, at the age of
forty-four. Nevertheless, Hardy re-emerged
in 1993 with a single, and—in addition
to becoming an astrology expert—has
been releasing records steadily ever since,
collaborating with the likes of Malcolm
McLaren, Iggy Pop, and Air.

WATCH

"Mon Amie la Rose"
There's a wealth of vintage Hardy footage on YouTube—this one captures her
coltish beauty most eloquently, but
also check out her "Les Garçons" duet
with Jacques Dutronc (whom she later
married and you can see why) for a
glimpse of her seldom-seen silly side.

DOWNLOAD "Qui Peut Dire"

WEAR

Motorcycle jacket
Andre Courreges designed au courant
fashions for Hardy to wear, and
Nicolas Ghesquiere of Balenciaga has
named her as a muse—but she never
looked more chic than when she was
wearing jeans and a leather jacket.

DUSTY SPRINGFIELD

London-born Mary O'Brien (nicknamed Dusty) formed the Springfields with her brother Dion and Tim Feild in 1960, changing her last name to match that of the group, and in 1963 she broke into the American charts with her solo single "I Only Want to Be With You"—one of the first hits of the British Invasion. The doe-eyed dollybird became a frequent guest on U.K. music show *Ready Steady Go!* and later had her own show, *It Must Be Dusty*, but as public taste turned away from the string-embellished pop epitomized by Burt Bacharach (many of whose songs Springfield sang the definitive versions of), her career slumped. Fascinated by American soul, she made a beeline south of the Mason-Dixon and in 1969 recorded what is widely acknowledged as her masterpiece, *Dusty In Memphis*. Springfield may not have been a songwriter, but she was masterful in her interpretations, using her husky voice to impart fragility and longing to every composition she sang (she also produced many of her own songs, though she was never credited). Called out as an influence by singers as diverse as Elton John (for whom she sang backup on "The Bitch Is Back"), Elvis Costello, and Cher, Springfield nevertheless spent much of the '70s and '80s in obscurity, struggling with drug addiction. In 1987 she collaborated with the Pet Shop Boys on "What Have I Done to Deserve This?" which relaunched her career before her death from cancer on March 2, 1999, the day before she was due to receive an OBE at Buckingham Palace, and just ten days before she was inducted into the Rock and Roll Hall of Fame.

HEAR

Dusty in Memphis (1969)
Consistently voted by music magazines as one of the greatest records of all time, this gem features "Son of A Preacher Man," a song Quentin Tarantino revived in 1994 when he included it on the *Pulp Fiction* sound track.

PRIMP

Black eyeshadow
After her 1970 disclosure that she was "perfectly as capable of being swayed by a girl as by a boy" to London's *Evening Standard*, Springfield became a bona fide gay icon—a status that was bolstered by her fondness for bouffant fire-hazard wigs (which she named after other pop singers), evening gowns, and exaggerated panda eye makeup.

DOWNLOAD "Son of a Preacher Man"

JANE

J'AIME MA POUPÉE ORANG-OUTANG /
ORANG-OUTANG, ORANG-OUTANG
— "ORANG-OUTANG"

WATCH

Blow-Up (1966)
No, it doesn't make
any sense. But it sure
does look pretty.

In 1968, gap-toothed gamine Jane Birkin was seduced by Galouise-smoking Frenchman Serge Gainsbourg, and *voilà*—history was made. English-born Birkin was only twenty-two and spoke little French when she met her forty-year-old musician co-star on the set of *Slogan* (she had already had a three-year marriage to famed English composer John Barry, who wrote the James Bond theme), but they were married within months. The young actress had already caused a *frisson* when she appeared nude in Antonioni's *Blow-Up*, but that was nothing compared to what followed when she and Gainsbourg released the song "Je T'aime Moi Non Plus" in 1969, a simple-but-saucy number he had originally written for previous girlfriend Bridgitte Bardot. Featuring explicitly orgasmic-sounding sighs courtesy of Miss Birkin, the scandalous song was banned in several countries and denounced by the Vatican, but it

BIRKIN

was also a huge hit, and in 1975 the couple made a film of the same name. Gainsbourg penned an extensive song repertoire for Birkin over the course of two decades, and their steamy creative partnership produced not only some of the sexiest and oddest French music ever, but also a daughter—Charlotte Gainsbourg, who has become a renowned actress and singer in her own right. (Her 2007 album *5:55* with Air is an understated beauty.) Birkin's younger daughter, Lou Doillon (fathered by her third husband, director Jacques Doillon), is now a model and style icon, taking a cue from mom, who was, of course, quite a progressive fashion plate in the '60s and '70s—in the '80s she had a famous (and famously expensive) Hermès handbag named after her, and back in the day she was known for parading around town with Gainsbourg wearing flesh-flashing dresses.

HEAR

Jane Birkin et Serge Gainsbourg (1969)
The couple's first musical outing *ensemble*. Birkin's thin, fragile singing voice is offset by Gainsbourg's suave baritone and buoyed by kitchy, kinky, orchestral pop.

Histoire de Melody Nelson (1971)
A twenty-eight-minute long concept album about an older man's love for a teenage girl ("played" by Birkin—one song features a recording of her being tickled by her brother), this is a sad, strange, and characteristically saucy record. When Gainsbourg died in 1991, Birkin buried him with the monkey she's holding on the cover.

PRIMP

Miller Harris L'Air de Rien, created for Jane Birkin
Translates as "the scent of nothing," which is appropriate, considering Birkin's propensity for public nudity.

NOW YOU AIN'T NOTHIN' BUT AN OLD TOM CAT, RUNNIN' AROUND MY HOUSE /
I'LL TELL YOU SOMETHING YOU OLD TOM CAT...YOU JUST LOST YOUR MOUSE
— "HOW DOES THAT GRAB YOU, DARLIN'?"

NANCY SINATRA

Even though the smokin'-hot '60s superstar inherited more than a little talent from her father, Frank, Nancy Sinatra was a late bloomer. She had released a whopping eleven flop singles on the Reprise label before—driven by their threats to end her contract—she sought out maverick songwriter/producer Lee Hazlewood. He became a mentor to young Nancy, coaxing her to sing in a lower key ("I wanted her to sing like a 16-year-old girl who screwed truck drivers," he later recounted) and vamp up her image. The result was a string of back-to-back hits kicked off with the good-humored camp classic "These Boots Are Made For Walkin'." With her blonde hair, frosted lips, heavy black eyeliner, and mod minidresses, Nancy brought a tough-chick cool to the '60s music scene that anticipated the liberated, down-and-dirty female singing of the next decade. Her collaborations with Hazlewood snuck cloaked S&M and drug references into mainstream pop, and their famous duet "Some Velvet Morning" is perhaps one of the darkest records ever to hit the Top 10. She definitely never hid from controversy though: her single "Kinky Love" was boycotted by radio stations due to its suggestive lyrics; her 1967 album, *Sugar,* was banned in Boston because the cover—featuring Nancy posing provocatively in a bikini—was considered obscene; and in 1995, with her father's blessing, she posed for *Playboy* (in boots, naturally). Unsurprisingly, Kim Deal and Kim Gordon (among many others) have proclaimed their love for her, as has Madonna, who once said, "One [of my two oldest fantasies] was to be Nancy Sinatra; the other was to be a nun."

HEAR

Movin' With Nancy (1968)
The sound track to Sinatra's Emmy Award-winning TV special, which was effectively a collection of pre-music-video music videos, marks the first appearance on record of the stunningly creepy "Some Velvet Morning," later covered by Primal Scream and Kate Moss.

Nancy Sinatra (2004)
A generation of musicians who grew up idolizing Nancy—including Jon Spencer, Pete Yorn, Thurston Moore, and Jarvis Cocker—were delighted to have her sing their songs. Morrissey's contribution, "Let Me Kiss You," provided the go-go-boot-clad goddess with her first hit in thirty years.

Boots LP (1969)
Definitive.

WATCH

The original *Boots...* video (1968)
Totally shagadelic.

PRIMP

False eyelashes
For a highly effective wink.

WEAR

White go-go boots "Are you ready boots? Start walkin'!"

TINA TURNER

The indomitable Ms. Turner has been dubbed the Queen of Rock 'n' Roll, and with good reason. Not only has this lady won countless Grammy Awards and sold more concert tickets than any other female singer in history, but her spitfire stage performances have been called out by the likes of Janis Joplin and Mick Jagger as crucial influences on their own live acts as well. Famously, Tina Turner didn't have an easy road to fame. Born Anna Mae Bullock to an African American father and Native American mother in 1939, she joined Ike Turner's soul revue at the age of eighteen, and soon after became his wife and the spotlight of the incendiary, screaming, shouting, jiggle-dancing road show that combined gospel fervor with unbridled sexuality. (If you want to see the very definition of a powerful, passionate performance, search out the pair doing "*Proud Mary*" on YouTube.) However, after years of enduring Ike's cocaine-fueled violent rages, Tina left him in the middle of a tour in 1976, with nothing but thirty-six cents and a gas card, a tale she recounted in her best-selling 1987 autobiography, *I, Tina,* which was made into an Academy Award-winning film in 1993, *What's Love Got to Do With It?* Tina spent a few years in the wilderness, scraping together money from small club tours and occasional TV appearances, until her 1984 album *Private Dancer* exploded onto the charts in one of the biggest comebacks in history. The music of Turner's '80s superstar days might have been far more polished and anodyne than her gritty R&B freak-out days with Ike, but the Queen herself was still a force of nature, with her electric-shock hair and, even in her sixties, legs that any twenty-year-old would kill for.

HEAR

Proud Mary: The Best of Ike and Tina Turner (1991) & *Dynamite* (1963)
Encompassing the pair's career from smokin'-hot early hits like "A Fool In Love" (Tina's first recorded vocal performance) to the Phil Spector–produced "River Deep, Mountain High," this is a great collection. Then seek out the reissue of 1963's *Dynamite*, which is exactly that.

WATCH

Mad Max Beyond Thunderdome (1985)
Check out Tina as the fierce Aunty Entity opposite a pre-cuckoo Mel Gibson. The movie's theme song, "We Don't Need Another Hero," was, at the time, inescapable.

WEAR

Stilettos
The lady doesn't do flats.

DOWNLOAD "Too Hot to Hold"

JANIS JOPLIN

The prototypical hard-living hippie-chick, Janis Joplin, unleashed her first scream in a Port Arthur, Texas hospital in 1943, and went on to light up the '60s like a comet. After a stint at the University of Texas in Austin, she made a beeline to join the liberal revolution happening in San Francisco's Haight-Ashbury district, a place whose freewheeling attitude she came to exemplify. In 1966 she joined a band called Big Brother & the Holding Company, performing with them at the Monterey Pop Festival in 1967, where her supercharged rendition of Big Mama Thornton's "Ball and Chain" abruptly catapulted her out of anonymity. From that moment on, Joplin was one of the biggest stars of the psychedelic era, especially with the release of the band's *Cheap Thrills* album (featuring cover art by R. Crumb), which boasted the barnstorming bravado of "Piece of My Heart." With her strands of beads, long disheveled hair, and penchant for flamboyant hair accessories, Joplin cut quite a figure on the music scene, and as the first white female rock singer to adopt the vocal and performance style of black R&B artists (along with her brashly liberal attitude toward sex and drugs), she was a pioneer who inspired many of her peers to write songs about her, including her one-time lover Leonard Cohen, who penned "Chelsea Hotel #2" about their affair. Unfortunately, her zealous taste for prodigious boozing and drug-taking finally caught up with her, and she was found dead of a heroin overdose in her room at the Landmark Hotel in Hollywood on October 4, 1970. Her hedonistic spirit persisted even to the end; she allocated money in her will for her friends to throw a big blowout after she died.

WEAR

Bell-bottom jeans
Drainpipes weren't an option for Joplin. And hey, you never know when you're going to need a place to stash your Jack Daniels.

Janis performing at Woodstock on YouTube.

HEAR

Pearl (1970)
Joplin was in the midst of recording this album (posthumously titled after her nickname) with her backing band Full Tilt Boogie when she OD'ed—the song for which she was to record vocals on the day that she died, "Buried Alive in the Blues," was left as an instrumental. Both the album and its single, "Me And Bobby McGee," were Number 1 hits.

DOWNLOAD "Try (Just a Little Bit Harder)"

WEAR

Full-body jumpsuit
Suzi was rarely seen
in anything other
than head-to-toe
leather or PVC.

SUZI QUATRO

PUT YOUR MAN IN THE CAN, HONEY /
GET HIM WHILE YOU CAN
— "CAN THE CAN"

HEAR

Can the Can (1973)
If this cover doesn't
make you want to
party, nothing will.

Born in Detroit in 1950 to jazz musician Art Quatro, Suzi formed her first band, the Pleasure Seekers, as a teenager, along with her sisters Patty, Nancy, and Arlene (Patty went on to start Fanny, the cult all-girl band, beloved by Bowie; Arlene married and had a daughter, Sherilyn Fenn, who starred in *Twin Peaks*). While playing with her subsequent band, Cradle, in 1970, Suzi was spotted by famed British record producer Mickie Most, who signed the screechy-voiced rocker to his label and brought her to England. Her first single, "Rolling Stone" was a flop everywhere but Portugal (where, oddly, it went to Number 1), but its 1973 follow-up, "Can the Can," struck gold. Suddenly the five-foot-tall singing bass player was the biggest female glam rock star in the U.K., a status cemented by the T.Rex-esque stomp of "Devil Gate Drive" and countless show-stopping appearances on *Top of the Pops*. Her star never shone as brightly in the States as it did in her adopted Blighty, but she did appear in seven episodes of *Happy Days* in '78 and '79 as Leather Tuscadero, the Fonz's girlfriend's rock 'n' roll little sis (show producer Garry Marshall reportedly sought her out for the role after seeing a poster of her on his daughter's bedroom wall). She was offered her own spin-off but declined, not wanting to be typecast. She went on to appear on stage in London's West End, host her own radio show, guest star on *Absolutely Fabulous*, and write a popular musical about Tallulah Bankhead.

PLAY

Status Graphite bass
When Suzi started
the Pleasure
Seekers, she
played bass only
because no one else
wanted to. It's
safe to say she
made it her own.

WATCH

Vintage footage of Suzi
performing "Your Mama
Won't Like Me" on
YouTube.

DOWNLOAD "Devil's Gate Drive"

BETTY DAVIS

HEAR

Betty Davis (1973)
On her sassy, stunning debut, Davis
wrote and produced all of her own
songs, and, prior to this record,
even penned the songs that got
the Commodores signed to Motown.

PRIMP

Styling pik
To keep that 'fro
super-freaky.

WEAR

Platform boots
Rick James,
who was a
huge fan
of Betty's,
would
have loved
these.

Born Betty Mabry in 1945, the future soul-funk dynamo first entered the public eye as a model before meeting jazz giant Miles Davis in 1966 and marrying him two years later. Betty introduced Miles to Jimi Hendrix and Sly Stone, prompting the musical innovations that would surface on his album *Filles de Kilimanjaro*, which had her photo on the cover, and the cosmic wig-out that was *Bitches Brew*. After the breakup of their marriage in 1969 (rumored to have been prompted by an affair with Hendrix), Davis started writing her own songs, the fruit of which appeared on her trailblazing 1973 self-titled debut, which featured members of Sly & the Family Stone and The Pointer Sisters. With her thigh-high metallic moon boots, Barbarella-esque outfits, and planet-sized afro, Davis telegraphed an ostentatious eroticism years ahead of its time. She sang and performed with ferocious energy, brazenly belting out lyrics about her sexual prowess—promising to seduce you, rough you up, and leave you pleading for more. After her last two albums floundered at the end of the '70s, however, she quietly disappeared, and was rumored to have moved to Pittsburgh and fallen into poverty. Miles said in the '80s, "If Betty were singing today she'd be something like Madonna, something like Prince…. She was the beginning of all that…." Her records were too extreme to win commercial success, but in 2007 they were finally re-released, reintroducing to the world the woman whose legacy paved the way for the likes of Missy Elliott, Lil' Kim, Macy Gray, and Kelis.

DOWNLOAD "Don't Call Her No Tramp"

TYPICAL GIRLS FEEL LIKE HELL / TYPICAL GIRLS WORRY ABOUT SPOTS, FAT, AND NATURAL SMELLS — "TYPICAL GIRLS"

THE SLITS

ARI-UP

Arianna Forster, a.k.a. Ari-Up, was born into a liberal, rock 'n' roll household in 1962—her German mother, Nora, was friends with Jimi Hendrix and later married Sex Pistol Johnny Rotten. Frequent houseguest Joe Strummer taught Ari how to play guitar, and, upon meeting Spanish-born drummer Paloma Romero, a.k.a. Palmolive, at a Patti Smith show when Ari was barely fourteen, the precocious punk rocker decided to start the Slits. After recruiting Tessa Pollitt, who picked up the bass for the first time two weeks before the Slits' debut show, and French guitarist Viv Albertine, who had previously played in a short-lived outfit called the Flowers of Romance with Palmolive and Sid Vicious, the band's lineup was complete, and they set about making such confrontational, dissonant, loud, and brash noise that the music world couldn't help but take notice. Although they were one of the last of the original wave of punk bands to land a record deal—no doubt because even within that aggressive, rebellious scene, the savage pandemonium of their shows was considered particularly shocking—they released their debut, *Cut*, in 1979 (just after Palmolive left to join another pioneering female punk band, the Raincoats). The now-trio appeared on the cover topless and smeared in mud against the backdrop of a pristine English garden, and the album itself was as rooted in experimental dub reggae as it was in punk, with songs such as "Typical Girls" characterized by choppy guitar, tribal rhythms, and Ari's screechy, off-key singing. The band followed up with the dark *Return of the Giant Slits* in 1981, but they split up shortly thereafter and Ari-Up decamped to Jamaica, where she became a clothing designer, raised three sons, and continued to perform under the name of Medusa. In 2006 Ari-Up and Pollitt re-formed the band with new members, producing a new EP, *Revenge of the Killer Slits*.

HEAR

Cut (1979)
This album is, to be honest, an acquired taste. But it's easy to hear in what ways the Slits' distinctively female and abrasively avant-garde approach influenced bands like Sonic Youth and the Riot Grrrl movement of the early '90s.

READ

England's Dreaming: Anarchy,
Sex Pistols, Punk Rock & Beyond
Jon Savage

Jon Savage's compre-
hensive history of the
most turbulent period in
British music foouses on
the Pistols, but paints a
vivid picture of the whole
spit-soaked scene the
Slits were immersed in.

WEAR

Tartan skirt
If you want to be
totally Ari-Up,
pair a punky plaid
miniskirt with huge
scary dreadlocks.

 DOWNLOAD "Typical Girls"

THE RUNAWAYS

WE'RE THE QUEENS OF NOISE / COME AND GET IT, BOYS — "QUEENS OF NOISE"

The Runaways may have been brought together by sleazy Svengali Kim Fowley, an L.A. producer who saw them as walking dollar signs, but these teenage girls rocked with a kind of raw power that can never be manufactured. Their best-known song, "Cherry Bomb," was written on the spot by fifteen-year-old Joan Jett, sixteen-year-old guitarist Lita Ford, and sixteen-year-old drummer Sandy West when singer Cherie Currie turned up for her audition (the lineup was later completed with Jackie Fox on bass). Infighting and mismanagement crippled the band's success, but they certainly turned a lot of heads during their short run. Each girl patterned her stage persona on her rock 'n' roll hero—Currie on David Bowie, Jett on Suzi Quatro, Ford on Deep Purple guitarist Ritchie Blackmore, West on Queen drummer Roger Taylor, and Fox on Gene Simmons—and with their bratty lyrics and heavy-metal-tinged, bass-heavy punk-rock sound, the girls stood out even when opening shows for the likes of Blondie, Cheap Trick, and the Ramones.

DOWNLOAD "Cherry Bomb"

Daring To Do It!

A CASABLANCA RECORD & FILMWORKS PRODUCTION
JODIE FOSTER · FOXES · SCOTT BAIO · SALLY KELLERMAN · RANDY QUAID
Produced by DAVID PUTTNAM and GERALD AYRES · Music by GIORGIO MORODER

WEAR

Gold spandex tights & platform boots
Sixteen-year-old Cherie's signature getup was a spandex jumpsuit with matching fingerless gloves and high-heeled boots—part Bowie, part Elvis, all rock 'n' roll.

WATCH

Foxes (1980)
With Jodie Foster, Scott Baio, a sound track by Giorgio Moroder that includes Donna Summer's "On the Radio" and tons of teen drinking and delinquency, the film in which Cherie made her acting debut (as an out-of-control, pill-popping—ahem—runaway) is a cult classic.

Joan Jett

HOW HAS BEING A WOMAN IN A BAND CHANGED OVER THE COURSE OF YOUR CAREER?

To be honest, it's always sucked in the business for girls. Back in the '80s after I left The Runaways, no one wanted to know me. I was eighteen and people were telling me I was a has-been. I sent out a demo to twenty-three record companies that had "I Love Rock 'n' Roll," "Do You Want to Touch Me?" and "Crimson and Clover" on it—and all of them passed. [Jett started her own label, Blackheart Records, in 1980.] So that just goes to show how much the record industry can tell if something's a hit. At first, people think it's cute—"Aww, she plays guitar!"—but if you're really serious, people get weird and nasty and call you scathing, cruel things, which really whacks away at a girl's self-esteem. I only know the rock side of it, but I bet it sucks for girls who want to be in pop music, too.

WHAT WAS IT LIKE WHEN YOU WERE IN THE RUNAWAYS?

At least then we were a gang—us against the world—we could lean on each other. We weren't making some big political statement, we were just girls who wanted to play rock music. But for many people at the time that was unthinkable.

HOW DID YOU INITIALLY GET INTO PLAYING MUSIC?

My parents told me I could do anything I wanted, so that helped. I was always in my bedroom playing along with T. Rex and Black Sabbath—stuff with big fat chords you could figure out yourself. Then my family moved out to California, and there was this club, Rodney's English Disco, for teenagers: no booze, but they played great records. I met Sandy West there—now she had balls. She used to hang out in the parking lot of the Rainbow Room at age fifteen to meet people in the record biz.

YOU'VE WORN SOME CRAZY STAGE OUTFITS. DO YOU HAVE A FAVORITE?

Yeah. Norma Kamali did some for me...there's one—a lace jumpsuit that I wore onstage for a whole year—that was completely see-through. Usually, I look back and shudder, but that was really cool.

HOW WOULD YOU SAY YOU'RE STILL INFLUENCING AND CULTIVATING YOUNG TALENT NOW?

I have a radio show, and I produce young punk bands. I use that term, punk, for lack of a better word because punk nowadays doesn't mean what it used to. It's diluted; everyone is punk. Everybody's a "rock star." But to me it still has an element of DIY and of realism. To me, it still means something edgy.

The Runaways (1976)
Fowley said he wanted "authentic slime," and he got it: This is a gritty, powerful party record. When Currie quit the band in 1977—she later married *Airplane!* star Robert Hays and appeared in *Foxes* and *This Is Spinal Tap* before opening an art gallery where she exhibits sculptures she creates using a chainsaw—Jett took over lead vocals for two more LPs, but this debut remains The Runaways' finest hour.

I Love Rock 'n' Roll (1981)
Jett emerged as the most successful solo musician after the band split, and this album was a sensation, spawning the definitive version of its title track (it was originally recorded by the Arrows in 1975, and...let's just forget the Britney cover ever happened).

PLAY

B.C. Rich Mockingbird guitar
Lita Ford's favorite

With her long, black bangs, sooty eye makeup, signature PVC trousers, and cocksure guitar stance, Chrissie Hynde is the ultimate rock chick. As a teenager, Hynde was electrified by the exotic energy of British Invasion bands such as the Rolling Stones and The Who, and she started her first band, Saturday Sunday Matinee (with Mark Mothersbaugh, who went on to mastermind Devo), while attending Kent State University, where she witnessed the infamous 1970 shooting of students by the Ohio National Guard. Obsessed with the music scene in England, she bought a one-way ticket to London in 1973, and within months she was writing for revered British music weekly *NME* as well as working as a shopgirl at SEX, Malcolm McLaren and Vivienne Westwood's bondage boutique on King's Road that was also an unofficial punk-rocker clubhouse. She played guitar with The Damned when they were still known as Masters of the Backside, but, too headstrong to be a supporting member in anyone else's band, she started the Pretenders in 1978. Soon after, they scored their first hit with "Stop Your Sobbing"—a cover of a Kinks' song. Hynde went on to have a daughter with Kinks frontman Ray Davies in 1983, and another in 1985 with Jim Kerr of Simple Minds, to whom she was married for six years. An adamant environmentalist and vegan whose outspoken anti-McDonald's, pro-marijuana views have sparked controversy over the course of her career, Hynde has lost none of her rebellious idealism even now that she's in her fifties. The woman who once said "I don't go for mainstream anything" will never be middle-of-the-road.

CHRISSIE HYNDE

I'M SPECIAL, SO SPECIAL /
I'VE GOTTA HAVE SOME OF YOUR
ATTENTION / GIVE IT TO ME
— "BRASS IN POCKET"

DOWNLOAD "Don't Get Me Wrong"

HEAR

The Pretenders (1980)
At a time when everyone else was making primal punk rock, the Pretenders were unafraid of being populist—their self-titled 1980 debut struck gold with its combination of pop prowess, classic songwriting, and Hynde's tough-but-tender lyrics. Here was a woman who would kick your ass if you wronged her, but whose sneering, swaggering attitude masked a heart of gold.

WEAR

Denim vest
In the early days, Hynde rocked denim vests with nothing underneath, and always looked totally tough.

Born in Chicago, Illinois, in 1946, Patricia Lee Smith worked in a factory as a teenager before making her way to New York City, where she began painting, writing for *Creem* magazine, and performing poetry readings at St. Mark's Poetry Project. Along the way, she met photographer Robert Mapplethorpe, and later moved into his apartment at the Hotel Chelsea. Smith and Mapplethorpe, whose relationship ambiguously blurred the boundaries of lovers and creative partners, became fixtures of the Warhol-scene stronghold Max's Kansas City, and it was Mapplethorpe who financed her first single, "Piss Factory / Hey Joe" in 1974. In the beginning Smith was more a beat poet who set her words to music than a rock star, but along with the New York Dolls and Television, she became one of the cornerstones of New York proto-punk, and a key player in the legendary, incendiary, CBGB scene. Smith's performances were notoriously intense: Dressed in her trademark androgynous menswear, she'd bellow free-form poetry that was set to dissonant, angry, three-chord rock 'n' roll supplied by her band. Smith has been called "the poet laureate of punk," and despite only scoring one hit single in her career—"Because the Night," which she co-wrote with Bruce Springsteen—you can hear her influence in everyone from PJ Harvey to Bat For Lashes to the Fiery Furnaces' Eleanor Friedberger. And when CBGB closed its doors forever on October 15, 2006, the revered venue chose Smith to headline on its final night.

PATTI SMITH

I'M GONNA GO ON THAT TRAIN AND GO TO NEW YORK CITY / I'M GONNA BE SOMEBODY — "PISS FACTORY"

WEAR

White button-down shirt
Patti could rock a button-down like no one else.

Patti Smith Horses

HEAR

Horses (1975)
When an album opens with the line "Jesus died for somebody's sins but not mine" you know you'd better buckle up. Smith's debut, produced by John Cale of the Velvet Underground and featuring an iconic portrait by Mapplethorpe on the cover, remains her quintessential work, a ferociously gritty statement of intent.

DOWNLOAD "Gloria"

DEBBIE HARRY

Debbie Harry is the ultimate icon. As the striking face and silvery voice of Blondie, she lit up the '70s and '80s with a nonchalant wit and tough-girl sex appeal that remains unrivaled to this day. Harry grew up in New Jersey with adopted parents (she used to fantasize that Marilyn Monroe was her birth-mother), and began her music career singing in a folk band called Wind in the Willows. Along the way, she worked as a Playboy bunny and a Max's Kansas City waitress, before meeting guitarist Chris Stein (who would become her long-term boyfriend) and starting Blondie in 1974. Although they emerged from the CBGB-centered punk scene, eclecticism was Blondie's calling card—they moved nimbly through New Wave, reggae, rap, and disco. Meanwhile, Harry has said that she created the enduringly cool Blondie persona by borrowing elements from Old Hollywood stars, '60s girl groups, and schlocky B-movies. She was a glamorous bombshell with an endearing edge—the devastating, icy effect created by her halo of platinum hair, unfeasibly high cheekbones, and limpid blue eyes was punctured by her gummy, dimpled smile and signature goofy zombie dance. The band split in 1982 when Stein became ill with a rare genetic disease, and Harry spent the next five years out of the spotlight, nursing him back to health. She went on to release solo albums, act in numerous films, and engage in various musical collaborations (notably with avant-garde group the Jazz Passengers) before the much-ballyhooed Blondie reunion in 1998.

Debbie Harry

WHAT DID YOU LISTEN TO WHEN YOU WERE A TEENAGER?

Well, I was a teenager quite a long time ago, so a lot of it was really early rock and R&B. That was a big influence on me. I liked Fats Domino a lot. And Elvis, oh boy. There weren't really rock bands; it was a whole different scene.

WHAT INSPIRED YOU TO GET INTO MUSIC YOURSELF?

Music just really turned me on. The stuff that Bob Dylan and Jimi Hendrix were doing really made sense to me and it was something I felt like I could do. In a way, I fell into it, and started out singing backup for other people.

THERE WEREN'T MANY WOMEN FRONTING BANDS AT THE TIME. WHOM DID YOU LOOK TO?

There was Janis Joplin, Grace Slick, and some English pop singers and girl groups…but that was about it.

WHAT WAS THE FIRST CONCERT YOU WENT TO?

I don't remember! As a teenager, I didn't go to concerts because a lot of them were in Brooklyn and it was too far for me to go from New Jersey, and I didn't really have any-body to go with. So I didn't really get to see any shows until I was in my early twenties.

HOW DID BLONDIE'S GENRE-JUMPING MUSICAL STYLE EVOLVE?

I think that I'm a product of radio, really—when I was growing up, stations were less specialized than they are now and some of the D.J.s were really on the money and really excited about new music, so they played everything. It was also just because we were such an urban band, and we had all grown up with so many different influences.

DID IT CONFUSE PEOPLE INITIALLY?

A bit. Audiences were really sophisticated, even back then, and for the most part they seemed to appreciate what we were doing. I think that the "punk" label was a stigma at first, because a lot of radio D.J.s and people in the press were very anti-punk—so a bit later in the '70s they came up with the term New Wave, which was much safer, more appetizing. But that was the biggest problem that we ever really faced, other than internally trying to reconcile the fact that as the lead singer, I was getting all of the attention.

WHAT WAS YOUR FIRST TOUR LIKE?

We went down to Australia where, weirdly, we had our first hit—and came up through Thailand and Japan and circled back through Europe. We did it on a wing and a prayer, believe me. We had no budget; we had a crew of two. It was pretty hairy.

AS A FASHION ICON YOURSELF, WHO ARE YOUR FASHION ICONS?

I like to watch what's happening on the streets. I think that in certain neighborhoods you can still see people who have a flair and a style of their own who are really making a statement. I look at that sort of thing more than I do designers.

DO YOU HAVE A FAVORITE BLONDIE VIDEO?

I think I like "Rapture" the best. That's hard to beat.

WATCH

Eat to the Beat (1979)
When Blondie released a "video album" along with this record, they were the first band ever to do so—foreshadowing pop music's embrace of all things multimedia. Both were reissued as a CD/DVD set in 2007.

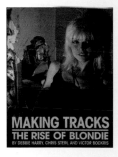

HEAR

Parallel Lines (1978)
As close to pop perfection as any album has come, cover art included.

READ

Making Tracks: The Rise of Blondie
Debbie Harry, Chris Stein, and Victor Bockris
From their gritty start to their glamorous heyday.

DOWNLOAD "Picture This"

Talking Heads: 77 (1977)
The band's debut prefigures pretty much every direction their music would later take: from the frantic, creepy "Psycho Killer" to the off-kilter romanticism of "Uh-Oh, Love Comes to Town," to the paranoid politics of "Don't Worry About the Government."

Tom Tom Club (1981)
Weymouth and hubby Frantz mixed art-rock with rap and bleepy, synth-heavy New Wave to create mammoth dance-floor hits like "Wordy Rappinghood" and "Genius of Love."

Tina Weymouth's unorthodox sense of rhythm was the bedrock of the Talking Heads' twitchy, driving post-punk sound, although the fact that she played bass was somewhat of an accident. Her first instrument was guitar, which she picked up at the age of fourteen but quickly abandoned—and, when she met David Byrne and drummer Chris Frantz (who she would later marry) at the Rhode Island School of Design in the early '70s, she was dedicated to the idea of becoming a painter. Nevertheless, when Byrne and Frantz started a band in New York after graduation (keyboardist and guitarist Jerry Harrison, formerly of the Modern Lovers, joined in 1976), she decided to try her hand at bass—and it was a revelation. Melding punk to funk to disco, Weymouth's basslines provided a polyrhythmic precision that set the Talking Heads apart from every other band at the time. Their first gig was opening for the Ramones at CBGB in 1975; soon they were playing regularly alongside such zeitgeist-defining bands as Blondie and Television. In 1977 they were signed to Sire Records and released their nervy debut, succinctly titled *Talking Heads: 77*, which was followed the next year by *More Songs About Buildings and Food*—a record that launched a highly creative partnership with producer Brian Eno that would continue through their next three albums. In 1981 Weymouth and Frantz started the Tom Tom Club, originally as a studio side-project. Later it became a full-fledged band, and their biggest hit, "Genius of Love," has been covered and sampled numerous times by everyone from Mariah Carey to Grandmaster Flash.

TINA WEYMOUTH

**I'M IN HEAVEN /
WITH THE MAVEN OF FUNK MUTATION
— "GENIUS OF LOVE"**

DOWNLOAD "Wordy Rappinghood"

POLY STYRENE
X-RAY SPEX

Born in London in 1957 to a British mother and Somali father, Marion Eliot was inspired to change her name to Poly Styrene and form X-Ray Spex after seeing a Sex Pistols show in 1976. She found her musical cohorts (including saxophonist Lora Logic, whose instrument was notably anomalous in the punk scene) by placing an ad in a local newspaper, and wrote all of the band's music. With her curly hair, braces, and penchant for wearing odd hats and clothes that she made herself, Poly Styrene was a punk rock precursor to the TV character Ugly Betty. (She once said, "If anybody tried to make me a sex symbol I would shave my head tomorrow.") And although she was supposedly trained as an opera singer, her delivery was all shrieks and screams—a vocal style that would greatly influence later vocalists like Yeah Yeah Yeahs' Karen O and The Gossip's Beth Ditto. The targets of her socially conscious lyrics were also years ahead of their time— she slammed everything from junk food to genetic engineering to society's obsession with youth ("Y'know it's a million dollar fear / If lines creep over here"). X-Ray Spex produced only one album before Poly dissolved the band in order to become a Hare Krishna devotee in 1979—the group did reunite briefly in the mid-90s, after Poly had released two solo albums, but the resulting album had little impact—yet her nonconformist, outspoken, DIY approach to music-making continues to resonate to this day.

HEAR

Germ Free Adolescents
(released in 1978; not released in the U.S. until 1992)
This forceful, attention-grabbing debut includes the group's one U.K. Top 30 hit, "The Day the World Turned Day-Glo," and "Oh Bondage! Up Yours!" which, judging by the frequency with which it is still played in New York City bars, has proved to be X-Ray Spex's most enduring track.

WATCH

Punk: Attitude (2005)
Don Letts's compelling documentary about the movement that changed music forever will make you want to stick a safety pin through your nose and go looking for a time machine.

DOWNLOAD "Oh Bondage! Up Yours!"

TAKE MY SHOES OFF AND THROW THEM IN THE LAKE /
AND I'LL BE TWO STEPS ON THE WATER
— "HOUNDS OF LOVE"

KATE BUSH

HEAR

Hounds of Love (1985)
Knocked Madonna's
Like A Virgin off
the top of the U.K.
charts. "Running Up
That Hill" was a hit
on American MTV, and
the album resulted
in a slew of Brit
Award nominations.

It's perfectly logical to be suspicious of a woman known for doing interpretive dances while wearing a unitard and singing in a glass-rattling soprano, but don't doubt Kate Bush. The madwoman-in-the-attic of British pop, she's truly one of the weirdest artists ever to crack the mainstream. Born in 1958 and raised in a farmhouse in Bexleyheath, Bush taught herself to play piano as a child, and was signed to EMI at the age of sixteen after being recommended by Pink Floyd's Dave Gilmour (a friend of the Bush family had given him a tape of her songs). The release of her debut single, "Wuthering Heights," in 1978 hit the world like a clap of thunder, and she became the first woman ever to have a self-written Number 1 hit on the U.K. charts. Known for her gothic subject matter and literary references (after Brontë, she went on to draw from the works of Tennyson, James Joyce, William Blake, and Hans Christian Anderson), her melodramatic, emotional, and high-pitched singing, and her eclectic musical style, which draws from everything from Celtic folk to prog-rock to New Wave, Bush produced most of her own albums and established a reputation as something of a hard-line perfectionist genius. She only toured once (in 1979), and after the release of her seventh album, *The Red Shoes*, in 1993, she disappeared from the public eye and devoted herself to raising her son. She resurfaced in 2005 with *Aerial*, a double album that achieved the holy trinity of rock music: artistically ambitious, critically acclaimed, and commercially successful.

WEAR

Spandex bodysuit
Kate studied
with the same
dance teacher
as David Bowie.
Even when she
looked like a
freaky mime, it
was all good.

READ

Wuthering Heights
by Emily Brontë
Because if you
haven't, you
should.

DOWNLOAD "Babooshka"

IN THE HEART OF THE NIGHT /
SHE SMILES LIKE MARDI GRAS /
SPINNING IN A DIZZY HAZE — "SHE'S A CARNIVAL"

SIOUXSIE SIOUX

Susan Janet Ballion, a.k.a Goth Goddess Siouxsie Sioux, got her start as a member of the Bromley Contingent, a group of teenagers (including Billy Idol) who followed the Sex Pistols around in the mid-'70s. Her fetish for fetish attire and her outrageous look—inspired by Nico, Patti Smith, and Catwoman—got her noticed everywhere she went. One important eye she caught was that of Malcolm McLaren, who drafted her at the last minute to play at the Punk Rock Festival he had organized in London's 100 Club in 1976—she didn't have anything to sing so she recited "The Lord's Prayer" over the raucous din of Sid Vicious bashing on drums behind her. Once Siouxsie and the Banshees became a proper band (their name was supposedly derived from Edgar Allan Poe's story "Cry of the Banshees"), Vicious was replaced by Budgie (real name Peter Clarke), whom Siouxsie later married; the couple has had a side-project, the Creatures, since 1981. Although Siouxsie has named comparatively conventional acts such as T. Rex, the Stooges, David Bowie, and the Doors as influences, the Banshees specialized in a sepulchral sound similar to that of the Cure (whose front man Robert Smith, incidentally, played guitar with the Banshees from 1982 to 1984). They struck a chord with gloom-lovers everywhere, and scored a major hit with the dance floor friendly "Peek-a-Boo" in 1981. The band's influence has been varied and long-lasting: U2, Ana Matronic of Scissor Sisters, Jane's Addiction, Tricky, Red Hot Chili Peppers, and Garbage have all credited their love of Siouxsie and the Banshees as being a formative factor in their own music.

WEAR

Bondage gear
Siouxsie used to wear a swastika armband to get attention. That's the only part of her look that you might not want to copy.

PRIMP

Smokey black eye makeup
Siouxsie's mask of makeup and drawn-on eyebrows are as dramatic as her music. Boo!

HEAR

Kaleidoscope (1980)
On which the Banshees started moving away from straight-up goth-punk and experimenting with electronic beats and Middle Eastern exotica.

DOWNLOAD "Christine"

HEAR

If You Love Me, Let Me Know (1974)
Olivia topped both the country and pop charts with this Grammy-winning album, and the single "I Honestly Love You" became her signature tune.

Physical (1981)
Oh spandex! Oh headbands! The title track spent ten weeks atop the *Billboard* charts, matching the record set by Debby Boone's "You Light Up My Life" for most weeks spent at Number 1 for a song by a female artist. Olivia simultaneously released a video album, which got a great boost from a new channel that debuted the same year: MTV.

WATCH

Xanadu (1980)
ELO + Olivia Newton-John. How can anything so wrong be so...right?

Some may remember her only as squeaky-clean Sandy in *Grease*, but Olivia Newton-John had a much more interesting career than her cheesed-out, '80s, headband-wearing heyday might suggest. Long before she exhorted the world to get physical, Newton-John produced some of the most winsomely beautiful radio hits of the '70s, and even won a Grammy Award in 1973 for Best Female Country Vocalist for her single "Let Me Be There." The granddaughter of Nobel Prize–winning physicist Max Born, Newton-John was born in England but raised in Melbourne, Australia, where she started a girl band, Sol Four, when she was fifteen. After winning a talent contest that took her back to England, she released her first single, "Till You Say You'll Be Mine" for Decca Records in 1966. She briefly joined a musical group called Toomorrow (put together by Don Kirshner, the man behind the Monkees), but soon set out on her own again, releasing her solo debut, *If Not For You* (with a title track written by Bob Dylan), in 1971, and scoring her first international hit. Her career hit supernova heights when John Travolta requested that she strut her stuff at his side in *Grease*, and she followed her character's transformation from good girl to bad girl in real life with her next album, *Totally Hot*, which featured her on the cover dressed in head-to-toe leather. Its follow-up, *Physical*, was so risqué it was banned in Utah, and she had to film an aerobics video to the title song in order to downplay the title track's overtly sexual subject matter. Our favorite Olivia moment, though, is her role as roller-skating muse Kira in the so-bad-it's-good 1980 musical *Xanadu*.

PRIMP

Blue eye pencil
Olivia was all about blue eye makeup and sheer lip gloss, but with her peaches-and-cream complexion, she could never hide her inner wholesomeness—even when she was all raunched out.

THERE'S NOTHING LEFT TO TALK ABOUT /
UNLESS IT'S HORIZONTALLY
— "PHYSICAL"

OLIVIA NEWTON-JOHN

DOWNLOAD "Deeper Than the Night"

THE GO-GO'S

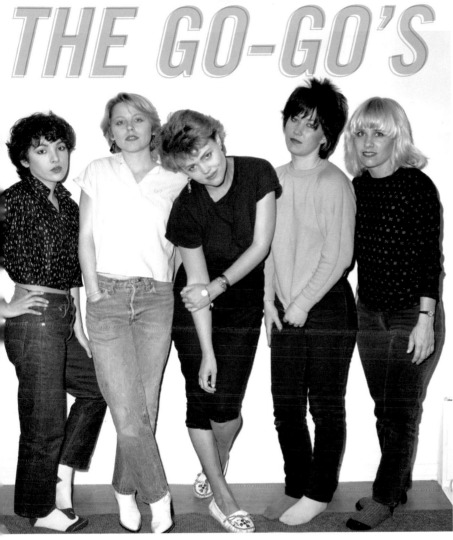

WEAR

Gigantic plastic earrings
The bigger
and brighter
the better.

HEAR

Beauty and the Beat
(1981)
Released just as
punk was giving
way to the radio-
friendlier sounds
of New Wave, *Beauty
and the Beat* was
a surprise hit
that put a pretty
face (or five) on
the underground
music scene for
people buying
their records at
tho local mall.
With songs about
bad boys and beach
parties—sung in
Carlisle's helium-
tinged vocals and
set to the band's
jittery beats—this
joyful, celebra-
tory record still
sounds fresh today.

WATCH

**The video for "Our
Lips Are Sealed" on
YouTube.**

The Go-Go's were born in 1978 in the grimy L.A. punk scene (singer Belinda Carlisle even briefly played drums with the Germs under the pseudonym "Dottie Danger"), but their unique surf guitar–driven pop-punk sound was their ticket out of the Valley. After opening for Madness in the U.K. in 1980, their single "We Got the Beat" was released on British punk label Stiff Records and became an underground club hit in the U.S. The following year their irrepressible debut album, *Beauty and the Beat*, earned the quintet—rounded out by guitarist Charlotte Caffey, drummer Gina Schock, bassist Kathy Valentine, and rhythm guitarist Jane Wiedlin—the honor of being the first all-woman band who wrote their own songs and played their own instruments to score a Number 1 album on the *Billboard* charts. Thanks to their boisterous live shows (in which Carlisle's arm-swinging, finger-snapping dance moves took center stage), kooky mix-and-match fashion sense, and indulgence in a rock 'n' roll lifestyle more hedonistic than that of many of their male peers, the Go-Go's managed to be both cool and glamorous. They began to splinter after their second album, *Vacation*, and disbanded in 1985, after which Carlisle went on to score mainstream pop hits and Wiedlin embarked on an acting career, appearing in, among other things, *Bill & Ted's Excellent Adventure*. The Go-Go's re-formed in 2001 to release a new album, *God Bless the Go-Go's,* the same year Carlisle posed for *Playboy* at the age of 42, saying, "You don't have to be age 20 and size 0 to be sexually viable or viable as a woman." Go, Go-Go, go!

DOWNLOAD "Skidmarks On My Heart"

STEVIE NICKS

HEAR

PLAY

Tambourine
Stevie always
wove ribbons
into hers for
added flair.

Fleetwood Mac
Rumours (1977)
The making of this
album is steeped
in rock 'n' roll
lore—not only was
there all kinds of
interband lovin' and
fightin' going on,
they were all coked
up to their eye-
balls. Creatively,
though, the group
was firing on all
cylinders—deserv-
edly, this is one
of the best-selling
albums of all time.

Stevie Nicks
Bella Donna (1981)
Solo Stevie in all
of her witchy-woman
wonderfulness—this
features the quint-
essential "Edge of
Seventeen," and
her classic duet
with the Eagles'
Don Henley (who was
briefly her lover),
"Leather and Lace."

With her raspy voice, velvet platform boots, and endless yards of billowing lace, and surrounded by the whiff of outlandish rumors of drug abuse (the ones about the long-gone septum are true; the ones about a dedicated assistant are not), Stevie Nicks has created both a larger-than-life persona and a career that has spanned more than three decades. Born Stephanie Lynn Nicks in Phoenix, Arizona, she joined Fleetwood Mac (with then-boyfriend Lindsey Buckingham) in the mid-'70s, and penned several of their biggest hits, including "Rhiannon," "Gold Dust Woman," "Landslide," and "Dreams." While still in the band, she also managed to have an equally-as-successful solo career with songs such as "Stand Back" and "Edge of Seventeen," and her divalike demands—including presidential suites and private jets—were notorious. Nicks has also been as famous for her white magic vibe as she was for her music: Crystal balls have appeared on four of her album covers, and her lyrics are peppered with references to witches and celestial bodies, while her signature dance move—a dramatic twirl—causes her trademark chiffon scarves and blonde hair to whip around her as if in an otherworldly wind. Her utterly unique style has even inspired Night of a Thousand Stevies, a seventeen-year-old annual party in New York where clubgoers, male and female, come decked in classic Stevie garb. Like the rock 'n' roll gypsy herself, its appeal is obvious.

WEAR

Long drapey sleeves, statement hats, and high-heeled boots
Best when made of crushed velvet or, of course, leather and lace.

DOWNLOAD "Stop Draggin' My Heart Around."

HEAR

In the Heat of the Night
(1979)
Benatar's saucy
debut, featuring
"Heartbreaker,"
"We Live for
Love," and a
cover of John
Mellencamp's "I
Need a Lover"
kick-started her
career and opened
the door for a
flood of female-
fronted pop and
New Wave acts.

KNOCK ME DOWN, IT'S ALL IN VAIN / I'LL GET RIGHT BACK ON
MY FEET AGAIN — "HIT ME WITH YOUR BEST SHOT"

PAT BENATAR

When MTV premiered in 1981, Pat Benatar—a sexy, spandex-clad, ball-busting bad-girl with a four-octave voice—was an instant smash (in fact, the video for "You Better Run" was the second ever played on the network, right after the Buggles' "Video Killed the Radio Star"). But Benatar wasn't an overnight success. Born Pat Andrzejewski in Greenpoint, Brooklyn in 1953, she grew up in Lindenhurst, New York, and married her high school sweetheart when she was only nineteen (who, fortunately, had the much more rockin' last name of Benatar), and worked as a bank clerk and waitress before she got her start singing in a Manhattan cabaret club. On Halloween 1977 she appeared onstage in a vampire costume that she had worn to a party earlier in the night, and the audience went wild—prompting her to realize that she needed a dramatic look to match her dramatic voice. In-spired by old sci-fi movies, she began to wear headbands, off-the-shoulder striped jersey tops, tight black leggings, and streaks of colorful makeup—thereby creating a look that not only defined the '80s but also propelled her through such classic rock–tinged pop hits as "Fire and Ice," "Treat Me Right," "Love Is a Battlefield," "We Belong," and "Hit Me With Your Best Shot" (picking up four Grammy Awards along the way). The hard and classic rock influences in her music set her apart from her poppier MTV peers, and her defiant, self-assured attitude defined Girl Power long before the phrase was even coined.

WEAR

Ankle boot
She may have had
an album called
Crimes of Passion,
but Pat never
perpetrated any
crimes of fashion.

PRIMP

Blush
Benatar, like
so many '80s
ladies, had
a tendency
to go a bit
bananas with
the blusher.
Smudge it lib-
erally across
cheekbones for
that "I just
won a dance-
off" glow.

DOWNLOAD "Heartbreaker"

"COME ON HOME GIRL,"
HE SAID WITH A SMILE /
"YOU DON'T HAVE TO LOVE ME YET,
LET'S GET HIGH FOR AWHILE"
—"MAGIC MAN"

HEART

HEAR

***Dreamboat Annie* (1976)**
***Little Queen* (1977)**
Heart at their heaviest. *Dreamboat Annie* sounds a lot like Zeppelin, and *Little Queen* kicks off with the kick-ass "Barracuda." What more could you need?

PLAY

HD-35 Nancy Wilson guitar by Martin
This limited edition, $3,500 guitar was designed by the queen of Heart herself.

The sisters Wilson—guitarist Nancy and singer Ann—are the heart of Heart, though the band was originally started by two brothers, Mike and Roger Fisher. When the Wilsons joined in 1974, it was immediately clear that these ladies would run the show, and within a year Heart were recording their debut, *Dreamboat Annie*, which spawned the howling, sexed-up "Crazy On You" and the darkly groovy "Magic Man." This was followed in '77 by the more psychedelic *Little Queen*, but after 1978's *Dog and Butterfly*, the band lost their solid gold touch—at least, until they made a major comeback in a flurry of big hair and even bigger hits in the mid-'80s. Nancy, who had a cameo as the "hot chick in a Corvette" in *Fast Times at Ridgemont High*, married director Cameron Crowe in 1986 and has since scored many of his films (including *Jerry Maguire* and *Almost Famous*); Ann released a solo album, *Hope & Glory*, in 2007. And despite their lower profile these days, Heart haven't stopped beating.

DOWNLOAD "Crazy on You"

TANYA DONELLY

HEAR

Throwing Muses
The Real Ramona
(1991)
Frantic guitars
and bizarre,
raw-boned lyr-
ics penned by
Hersh, who was
struggling with
mental illness
at the time,
characterize
Throwing Muses'
most accom-
plished album.

The Breeders
Pod **(1990)**
Donelly recorded
the Breeders'
debut—a twisted-
but-catchy album
with menacing
melodies, occa-
sionally abrasive
vocals, and
graphic subject
matters—with Kim
Deal in Scotland
while the Pixies
bass player was
on hiatus from
a tour (Perfect
Disaster's
Josephine Wiggs
and Slint
drummer Britt
Walford also
contributed).

Tanya Donelly's dainty, blonde looks and cookie-sweet, little-girl voice belie her gutsy guitar-playing and deft lyricism, talents she put to use as a founding member of a holy trinity of '90s girl-fronted indie bands—the Throwing Muses, the Breeders, and Belly. She and her stepsister Kristin Hersh launched Throwing Muses in their Newport, Rhode Island garage when they were only fifteen years old, self-releasing an EP in 1984 that resulted in the band becoming the first American act to be signed by cult British label 4AD. Their off-kilter guitar pop and distinctively idiosyncratic approach to songwriting propelled them through five years and five college-radio-hit albums before Donelly, frustrated by Hersh's dominance in the band, quit. She had already moonlighted with the Pixies' Kim Deal on the Breeders debut in 1990, but Belly, which she started in 1991, was the first project that was entirely her own. With Belly, Donelly attained com-mercial success to match her critical acclaim when the band's million-selling debut, *Star*, was nominated for two Grammy Awards. After their second album belly-flopped in 1995, however, she split up the band and struck out on her own. Always uncomfortable with the limelight, she married former Juliana Hatfield Three bassist Dean Fisher in 1996, and has since been quietly releasing low-key solo albums.

Belly
Star **(1993)**
Striking for its
juxtaposition
of the nice and
nasty—a mesh of
hazy guitars and
Donelly's blithe-
ly chirpy vocals
sugarcoat dark,
often creepy
lyrics, which
are loaded with
fairy-tale images
and obscure sym-
bolism. A super-
weird—and truly
great—record.

DOWNLOAD "Feed the Tree"

The Pixies
Doolittle **(1989)**
Everyone on the planet should own every Pixies album ever made. But if you have to choose just one, make it *Doolittle*.

The Breeders
Last Splash **(1993)**
In addition to her ballsy bass playing, Deal's surprisingly lovely, pristine voice and batty lyrics make this an indie-rock-to-MTV crossover classic.

KIM DEAL

I'LL BE YOUR WHATEVER YOU WANT /
THE BONG IN THIS REGGAE SONG
— "CANNONBALL"

DOWNLOAD "Fortunately Gone"

Kim Deal and her twin sister Kelley (born June 10, 1961, in Dayton, Ohio) formed their first band while in high school, playing at local truck stops. In 1985, one week after moving to Boston with then-husband John Murphy, Deal answered a newspaper ad that read: "Looking for a female bassist, high harmony, must like Hüsker Dü, Peter, Paul & Mary, no chops." Despite never having played bass and not actually owning one (she arrived at the audition empty-handed), she was still inducted into the newly formed Pixies by front man Black Francis because she was the only one who turned up. Her style was tomboy schlep, her attitude all cigarette-smoking nonchalance, but Deal was a force to be reckoned with—she helped create the Pixies' distinctive, twisted surf-punk sound, and, of course, sang on several of their most memorable tracks, such as "Gigantic." The band's influence on '90s alt-rock can never be overestimated—but as Francis began to completely hog songwriting duties on their later albums, Deal became disenchanted. She had recorded the Breeders' first album as a side-project with Tanya Donelly, and after the Pixies split in 1993, she made the band a full-time project (drafting her sister to play guitar), subsequently scoring a major hit with 1993's "Cannonball." Deal, who has since kept the Breeders going, along with a side-project called the Amps and the re-formed Pixies, is one of the most unilaterally adored bass players ever: As the Dandy Warhols sang in 1997, "Here's what I feel / Just want a girl as cool as Kim Deal."

PRIMP

Brown hair powder
For when you're just too rock 'n' roll to shampoo. A must for the tour bus.

47

WHAT ARE YOU GONNA DO FOR ME? /
I MEAN, ARE YOU GONNA LIBERATE US GIRLS
FROM MALE WHITE CORPORATE OPPRESSION?
— "KOOL THING"

KIM GORDON

WATCH

1991: The Year Punk Broke (1992) Sonic Youth's seminal on-the-road documentary is like a time capsule: Gordon dances with Kurt Cobain on a railroad track, and Moore utters his famous decree: "You are humans, go forth and thrash!"

Honestly, what hasn't she done? Experimental rock's reigning bass-and-guitar-playing queen is also an accomplished multi-media artist and curator, clothing designer, music-video director, actress, model, producer, feminist, and all-around muse—all while sustaining, with Thurston Moore, one of the longest and most fruitful creative and romantic partnerships in music. Gordon grew up in California but moved to New York in 1980 with an art degree and wrote for *ArtForum* magazine for a while before forming Sonic Youth in 1981 with Moore, originally inspired by the post-punk No Wave movement. In breaking completely with songwriting conventions and detuning their instruments to create feedback-heavy, droning soundscapes, Sonic Youth became major players in the downtown art-rock scene and laid the groundwork for innumerable alt-rock bands to follow. Gordon—who has branched out with a number of side projects, most notably Free Kitten (with Boredoms' Yoshimi and Pussy Galore's Julie Cafritz)—is a firecracker onstage, whether she's walking on her bass in high heels or flailing her arms and blonde hair in a cathartic dervish-dance. She may now be in her fifties, but as anybody—male or female—will confirm, she's still totally hot.

Kim Gordon

A LOT OF GIRLS ARE DRAWN TO PLAYING BASS OVER GUITAR OR DRUMS—WHY DO YOU THINK THAT IS?

It's weird, because it is kind of a supportive role, but then it's also not. It is very defining in terms of holding all of the music together, and kind of not defined in a certain way. I could go really in depth and compare it to female sexuality in terms of it being nonphallic, but I'll stop myself. In a way it is [the most glamorous instrument], because it's mysterious. And obviously you don't have to be in the spotlight directly. One of the reasons why I got into wanting to play initially was because I was writing about male sexuality and male bonding in music. One of the first things I wrote was called "Trash, Drugs, and Male Bonding" for this art magazine called *Real Life*, and I felt like I wanted to be in the middle of it, instead of being a voyeur looking from the outside in. And playing bass gives you kind of a backseat perspective.

WHO WERE YOUR ROLE MODELS EARLY ON, AS FAR AS PERFORMING WENT?

I remember there were women like Lydia Lunch and Siouxsie and the Banshees and the Slits who had these personas, and were so glamorous, and I thought there is no way I could be like that. It was hard to reconcile, but then luckily, even though the milieu of hardcore was very "boy," it was more about being who you were. So I was able to then say, I'm just going to be myself and make music and maybe girls will relate to that. I'm not going to try to be this exotic creature or something.

DO YOU HAVE FAVORITE THINGS THAT YOU'VE WORN ONSTAGE?

Oh yeah. I had this great Marc Jacobs dress: It was blue sequins and it was great because it was sort of flapper-ish but you couldn't really tell what it was, like, was it a dress or what? And also this dress…it was almost like a tennis dress, it was really simple, but then it had this long pink-net skirt that wrapped around it. I also have a gold Philip Lim dress that I really like—but I took it to the dry cleaner recently and all the gold came off.

SONIC YOUTH IS A RARE EXAMPLE OF A BAND THAT HAS NOT ONLY MAINTAINED A LONG CAREER BUT HAS CONTINUED TO PUT OUT GREAT RECORDS—WHAT'S THE SECRET?

Maybe we just put in a little more effort! We listen to different kinds of music, which keeps things going, and maybe it's because we never became really big; we just held steady. It's also the way we do what we do: It's a whole lifestyle.

ARE THERE ANY RECORDS THAT YOU CONSIDER YOUR ALL-TIME FAVORITES?

Oh wow. That is a tough question. I guess DNA's *A Taste of DNA*, PiL's *Metal Box*, and the Slits, *Cut*. They had a really big impact on me—just girls playing amazing music and really having fun.

HOW HAVE YOUR SOURCES OF INSPIRATION CHANGED OVER THE YEARS?

Lately I've been listening to '60s folk music. When I was growing up, I listened to Dylan and Neil Young and went up to the Filmore to see bands, so I've been returning a little bit to Buffalo Springfield and groups like that. Maybe it's my nostalgia for California coming out. But I'm not listening to hardcore music anymore.

DOWNLOAD "Bull in the Heather"

Daydream Nation (1988)
Widely praised as Sonic Youth's masterpiece, *Daydream Nation* is a tour de force that tautly balances the band's dissonant freak-outs with hypnotically beautiful melodies.

Goo (1990)
Sonic Youth is the gold standard example of an underground band that signed to a major label without sacrificing their sound, and *Goo*, their first album on Geffen Records, is an exercise in punk-rock simplicity, from the Dr. Suess-esque title track to the hilariously wonderful "Mildred Pierce" (The song's only lyrics: "Mildred! Mildred Pierce! Nooooo! Mildred Pierce! Whyyyyy?!").

WEAR

Built By Wendy guitar strap & miniskirt
Gordon is adamantly not one of the boys, as her cute onstage ensembles never fail to demonstrate.

LIZ PHAIR

EVERY TIME I SEE YOUR FACE
I GET ALL WET BETWEEN MY LEGS /
EVERY TIME YOU PASS ME BY
I BREATHE A SIGH OF PAIN — "FLOWER"

HEAR

Exile in Guyville (1993) Phair's seminal release remains unlike anything recorded before—or since.

She couldn't actually sing very well, but that was part of the point. Liz Phair's DIY debut album, *Exile in Guyville,* a song-by-song response to the Rolling Stones' *Exile on Main Street,* blew a hole in the side of the male-dominated indie scene with its frank expressions of female lust—she could be just as dirty, if not dirtier, than the boys, while also being honest, raw, and vulnerable. Phair never set out to be a star, though. She was selling drawings on the streets of Chicago to support herself (she had an art degree from Oberlin College) when a friend heard her rudimentary guitar-playing and dared her to record a demo. Her response was to make what she called the *Girly Sound* tapes, cassettes containing thirty-two songs that she laid down in her bedroom on a 4-track machine and then gave to friends. One of these tapes made its way to a Matador Records A&R man, who offered Phair $3,000 to record a single. Instead, she stretched the money to pay for all of the eighteen tracks that became *Guyville.* Released in 1993, the album was smart, funny, refreshingly unpretentious, and, at the time, incredibly shocking—audiences had never heard a girl sing lines like "I want to be your blow job queen" or "I want to f— you like a dog." Phair's follow-up, *Whipsmart,* included a single, "Supernova," that became a *Billboard* Top 10 hit with rotation on MTV, but the singer's anti–self-promotion stance, coupled with a debilitating case of stage fright, meant that she never really cashed in on the commercial success within her grasp. When she did try to relaunch her career in 2003 with the high-gloss, self-titled *Liz Phair,* wearing belly-baring shirts and employing Avril Lavigne's production team, a generation of indie-rock girls wept.

DOWNLOAD "Fuck and Run"

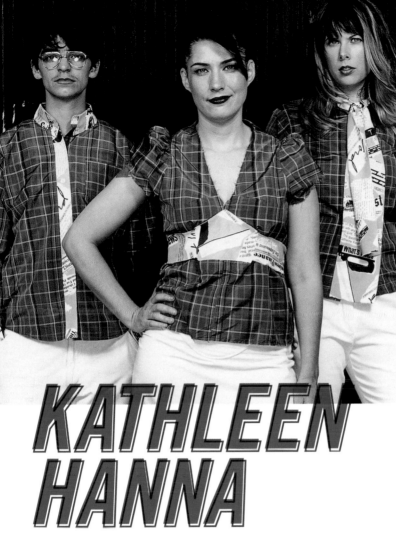

WHEN SHE TALKS, I HEAR THE REVOLUTION
— "REBEL GIRL"

KATHLEEN HANNA

As much an icon in zine culture and feminist activism as she is in music, the fact that Kathleen Hanna isn't a household name is a damn shame (tellingly, when her name came up in a party scene in one episode of *The L Word*, only the lesbians in the room knew who she was). In the early '90s, Hanna's all-girl band Bikini Kill, which she started with Tobi Vail and Kathi Wilcox while in college, was a major force in the same Olympia, Washington punk scene that spawned Nirvana (in fact, Hanna dated Dave Grohl for a while, and a phrase she spray-painted on Kurt Cobain's wall one night—"Kurt Smells Like Teen Spirit"—inspired the band's most famous song). Bikini Kill's principles—political awareness, DIY, and the importance of female support and community—kick-started the Riot Grrrl movement, which was named after a zine started by members of the band Bratmobile and to which Hanna contributed. Initially a response to the sexism in the underground West Coast music scene, Riot Grrrl (the movement) became a call to action to increase female involvement in punk rock, inspiring everyone from Sleater-Kinney to Courtney Love and The Gossip's Beth Ditto to rock out. After releasing a solo album under the name Julie Ruin in 1998, Hanna went on to form Le Tigre in New York City with Johanna Fateman in 1998. Calling themselves "underground electro-feminist performance artists," they released three albums before disbanding in 2007, a year after Hanna—lucky girl—married Ad-Rock from the Beastie Boys.

DOWNLOAD Le Tigre's "Hot Topic"

HEAR

Bikini Kill
The CD Version of the First Two Records (1992)
Le Tigre
Le Tigre (1999)
The two ends of the Hanna spectrum—raw, gutsy punk rock and sample-heavy protest-pop. Both are whip-smart, ferociously pissed-off and, thankfully, also fun to dance to.

READ

The Feminine Mystique
Betty Friedan
When she was nine, Hanna's mother took her to see Gloria Steinem speak at a rally. Shortly thereafter, she checked this book out of the library—and a Riot Grrrl was born.

COURTNEY LOVE

WATCH ME BREAK
AND WATCH ME BURN
— "MISS WORLD"

SID & NANCY

WATCH

Sid and Nancy (1986)
Love made an infamous
audition video for
this movie about the
doomed punk paramours
in which she threat-
ened to kill the pro-
ducers if they didn't
give her the role of
Nancy. Impressed but
unfazed, they cast
her as one of Nancy's
junkie friends.

HEAR

Live Through This (1994)
A bit-dated now,
but still kicks
some serious ass.

Celebrity Skin (1998)
Beneath its
glossy production
lies serious,
and affecting,
darkness.

PRIMP

Red lipstick
After missing
your mouth,
use it to
write slogans
on your chest.

Courtney Love has been many things—groupie, Riot Grrrl, widow, movie star, rock star, drug addict—and she is both loved and hated because of it. Born Courtney Michelle Harrison in 1964, she spent her childhood being shuffled between hippie communes, boarding schools, and foster families. A social worker in a juvenile hall turned her on to British punk rock by giving her a Sex Pistols record and at the age of fifteen, she emancipated herself from her family and traveled to England where she lived with musician Julian Cope for a while before returning to the U.S. She landed a role as Nancy Spungen's abrasive best friend in *Sid and Nancy* in 1986, appeared in the music video for the Ramones' "I Wanna Be Sedated," and started and abandoned (or was kicked out of) many bands, including Babes in Toyland and Faith No More, before starting Hole in 1989. The band released their Kim Gordon-produced debut *Pretty On the Inside* in 1991, the same year Love met Kurt Cobain at a Butthole Surfers gig. They were married in 1992, and their daughter Frances Bean was born that August. That was where the good times ended: Cobain killed himself on April 5, 1994, one week before the release of Hole's break-through second album *Live Through This,* and just two months later, the band's bassist Kristen Pfaff died of a heroin overdose. Love has experienced a roller-coaster ride of ups (most famously in her transformation into glamorous starlet and knockout performance in 1996's *The People Vs. Larry Flint*) and downs in the years since, not to mention enough court-ordered rehab attempts to rival Pete Doherty. Nevertheless, if nothing else, her fiery, opinionated outbursts and tendency to strip in public will always have people watching to see what she does next.

READ

Dirty Blonde: The Diaries of Courtney Love by Courtney Love For a glimpse inside her crazy, crazy mind.

WEAR

Baby-doll dress and little-girl barrettes She looked like a demented toddler, but in the '90s, everybody copied Love's look.

DOWNLOAD "Malibu"

Justin Timberlake grabbed it during an awards show performance. The British public voted it Rear of the Year in a 2003 newspaper poll. Kylie Minogue's butt is an asset nearly as famous as the pint-sized star it's attached to, and she, like Madonna and McDonald's, is an institution. Ever since she boogied her way out of Australia (where she was already a famous actress on the soap *Neighbours*) with the hit single "Locomotion" in 1987, she has been a coquettish chameleon capable of infusing even the most vapid pop songs with adorableness. Her relationship with INXS singer Michael Hutchence and second album *Rhythm of Love* helped vamp up her squeaky-clean image a bit in 1990, but Kylie still had a long road to travel before she gained any kind of credibility—although her 1995 murder ballad, "Where the Wild Roses Grow," with goth-king Nick Cave certainly helped. Another reinvention came with 2000's disco-inflected *Light Years*, followed by the electro-pop *Fever* in 2001. The lead single, "Can't Get You Out of My Head," hit Number 1 in forty countries around the globe and was followed by a lavish world tour (Kylie's sets and costumes are so extravagantly fabulous they have been exhibited at the Victoria and Albert Museum in London). A multitasking dynamo, Minogue has her own fragrance and clothing line, and has sidelined as a children's book author, an H&M model, and actress; and her recovery from breast cancer in 2006 makes the woman John Galliano once described as "a blend of Lolita and Barbarella" even more of a heroine.

DID I FORGET TO MENTION
THAT I FOUND A NEW DIRECTION /
AND IT LEADS BACK TO ME?
— "SPINNING AROUND"

KYLIE MINOGUE

Ultimate Kylie (2004)
A collection of Kylie's most memorable videos released concurrently on CD and DVD. Watch out for "Slow," in which swimsuit-clad men do slo-mo pelvic thrusts while she rolls around languorously on a beach towel.

HEAR

Fever (2001)
Fizzy, fun, and relentlessly dance-tastic. Definitely Kylie at her hottest.

WEAR

Hot pants
Kylie's "Spinning Around" video introduced the world to a pair of gold hot pants that later became the centerpiece of a V&A exhibition.

PRIMP

Murad Firm and Tone Serum
Kylie probably doesn't need any help, but for those not naturally blessed with perfectly pert posteriors, there's this.

DOWNLOAD "Can't Get You Out of My Head"

BJÖRK

Many musicians call themselves "artists," but Björk (who doesn't use her last name, Gudmundsdottir, professionally, for obvious reasons) is the real deal. By the time she released her remarkable solo album *Debut* in 1993, she had already been making music for fifteen years in her hometown of Reyjavík with five separate bands (including an all-girl punk band called Spit and Snot that she formed when she was fourteen, and Tappi Tíkarrass, which translates from Icelandic as "Cork the Bitch's Ass"). Of these only the Sugarcubes, a product of the arts collective Smekkleysa (Bad Taste), had achieved any mainstream success with the international hit single "Birthday" in 1990. Following the success of *Debut*, which went platinum in the U.S., the pixielike singer released *Post*, to which trip-hop maestros Nellee Hooper of Massive Attack and Tricky contributed their production skills; then, in 1997, came what many critics consider her masterpiece, *Homogenic*. Around this time, Björk also enlisted Michel Gondry and Chris Cunningham to direct her music videos, displaying a keen visual sensibility that has characterized her career. An occasional actress, Björk won the best actress award at Cannes in 2000 for her role as a blind factory worker in Lars von Trier's *Dancer in the Dark*, and in 2005 appeared opposite her boyfriend Matthew Barney in his experimental *Drawing Restraint 9* (she also released sound tracks for both films). Truly, she's at the vanguard of every medium she touches.

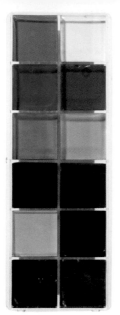

PRIMP

HEAR

Debut (1993)
The songs on this album—the beautiful "Venus as a Boy," the giddy "Big Time Sensuality"—remain some of her most intimate and intoxicatingly joyful.

Homogenic (1997)
A vast, ambitious album that dispelled images of the cutesy, impish girl of "It's Oh So Quiet" (the surprise hit from *Post*) and includes such memorable tracks as "Jóga," "All Is Full of Love," and "Bachelorette."

WEAR

Anything you damn well please
Remember the swan dress?

DOWNLOAD "All Is Full of Love"

BE KIND TO ME, OR TREAT ME MEAN / I'LL MAKE THE MOST OF IT,
I'M AN EXTRAORDINARY MACHINE — "EXTRAORDINARY MACHINE"

FIONA APPLE

HEAR

Tidal (1996)
An angsty firebrand
of a teenager,
Apple bashed out
her frustrations on
the piano and came
up with songs that
radiated wisdom and
sophistication far
beyond her years.
Recorded after a
demo tape she made
while still in
high school found
its way into the
hands of a Sony
label executive,
Tidal gets better
with age, much
like Apple herself.

**Extraordinary Machine
(2005)**
Recorded twice,
with two differ-
ent producers, and
famously shelved
for a time until
her fans rallied
for its release,
this album—with its
witty, redemptive
lyrics and jazzy,
curiously wonky time
signatures—solidifies
Apple's standing as
a unique talent.

Fiona Apple is among the most fierce-willed and creatively autonomous female singer-song-writers of her generation—and one who has managed to maintain her cult credibility despite mainstream success. Born Fiona Apple McAfee Maggart in 1977 into a family with entertainment roots stretching back to the vaudeville era, she endured a difficult childhood (including a rape at the age of twelve), which fed into the highly articulate, emotionally charged lyrics of her precocious 1996 debut, *Tidal*, released when she was nineteen. The album caused a stir not only for Apple's troubling backstory but also for a Mark Romanek–directed video of its most successful single, "Criminal," in which the waifish singer drifted around a dark apartment in nothing but her underwear. An outburst during her acceptance speech for Best New Artist at the 1997 MTV Music Awards—in which she admonished fans not to emulate anyone onstage that night because "this world is bullshit"—also gave her a reputation for being a loose cannon. But Apple refused to be pigeonholed or victimized by her detractors, a defiant attitude that was exemplified in 1999 by her second album, which she named with a ninety-word poem (shortened to *When the Pawn...*) that entered the *Guinness Book of World Records* as the longest album title in history. Plagued by difficulties with her label, it took six years for Apple to release her next album, *Extraordinary Machine*—a triumphant work that showcases her smoky, contralto vocals and torch song–inspired melodies to beguiling effect. The fact that it became the highest-charting album of her career so far is a perfect Apple-esque middle finger to The Man.

PRIMP

Bed Head Mastermind
Because beauty-wise, Apple's
main event is always her mane.

DOWNLOAD "Parting Gift"

JUSTINE FRISCHMANN

I'D WORK VERY HARD
BUT I'M LAZY / I'VE GOT
A LOT OF SONGS BUT
THEY'RE ALL IN MY HEAD
— "WAKING UP"

When Britpop ruled the U.K. in the mid-'90s, Justine Frischmann and then-boyfriend Damon Albarn of Blur were the scene's king and queen. Tomboyish and elegant, Justine was tough and mysterious, with a low, insouciant speaking voice and a penchant for wearing head-to-toe black. She had been a founding member of Suede with previous boyfriend Brett Anderson (she named the band and played lead guitar), but left when their relationship ended, starting Elastica in 1993 with red-haired siren Donna Matthews on guitar, perpetually scowling bassist Annie Holland, and Justin Welch, the token boy, on drums. The band's taut, angular New Wave sound recalled bands such as Blondie, the Stranglers, the Buzzcocks, and Wire (in the latter case so much so that they were sued by Wire's management), but their perfunctory two-minute blasts of buzzy guitars and sharp-witted lyrics were gripping and thrilling in a way that was entirely their own. As a result, Elastica's self-titled first album—bolstered by such stingingly infectious songs as "Stutter" (about a lover who can't get it up) and "Line Up" (a snarky put-down of rock groupies)—entered the U.K. charts at Number 1, and became the country's fastest-selling debut ever. Its follow-up, however, was five years in the making, as the band's early progress became complicated by drug use and infighting (Holland and Matthews both eventually quit). By the time *The Menace* finally appeared in 2000, public enthusiasm had cooled. Justine, who had always been uncomfortable with her own notoriety, announced Elastica's official demise shortly thereafter. Since then she has hosted TV shows about architecture and art for the BBC, and co-wrote and produced demos for former roommate M.I.A.'s debut album *Arular*, but she has vowed never again to return to the music scene fronting a band.

HEAR

Elastica (1995)
Frischmann and Matthews rifled through their late '70s and early '80s record collections for inspiration, then set about writing this, one of the most flawless and concise debut albums of all time.

The Menace (2000)
Unfairly derided upon its release, this album is patently a half-assed effort compared to its predecessor, but nevertheless it has its high points, including a characteristically cantankerous contribution from The Fall's Mark E. Smith on "How He Wrote Elastica Man," and the explosive, electronica-lashed "Generator."

WEAR

Doc Martens
At the height of Britpop, Justine had the world at her feet. And those feet were wearing Doc Martens.

DOWNLOAD "Connection"

MISSY ELLIOTT

GIRLFRIEND WANNA BE LIKE ME,
NEVER / YOU WON'T FIND A BITCH
THAT'S EVEN BETTER / I MAKE YOU
HOT AS LAS VEGAS WEATHER
— "WORK IT"

She runs her own record label. She has collaborated with everyone from Timbaland (whom she's known since she was fifteen) to Madonna; from M.I.A. to Janet Jackson. She's had her own TV show and clothing label (with adidas), won multiple VMAs and Grammy Awards, written the script for a movie about her life, released seven albums, and is the biggest-selling female rapper of all time. And for Missy Elliott, that's just the tip of the iceberg. Growing up in Portsmouth, Virginia, Elliott endured a difficult, abusive childhood (she wrote fan letters to Michael and Janet Jackson, begging them to come save her), which she escaped as a teen when she formed the R&B group Sista and moved to New York. Their Timbaland-produced debut LP, 1994's *All the Sistas Around the World*, was shelved by their label, but that didn't stop Missy. She started writing and producing for other artists, then founded The Goldmind, Inc., on which she released her solo debut *Supa Dupa Fly* in 1997. Since then—as a rapper, singer, songwriter, MC, and producer—she has become one of the most consistently creative and inspiring artists working today, blurring the boundaries between dance, R&B, hip-hop, pop, and rock, and breaking down barriers and stereotypes at every turn.

MISSY ELLIOTT

PRIMP

Lipgloss
Missy's lips drip with words of wisdom—and lots of high-shine gloss.

HEAR

Under Construction (2002)
If you don't yet own a Missy record, make this the first (unless you can pick up her greatest hits, *Respect M.E.*, on import). Chances are this won't be the last, as Missy—who has called herself "so addictive"—would be the first to tell you.

WEAR

Sneakers
adidas, naturally.

DOWNLOAD "Lose Control"

HEAR

Public Warning (2006)
Tough stuff—and
funny, too.

Pint-sized but pugnacious, Lady Sovereign—born Louise Amanda Harman in 1985—has beat the odds to become the first of her kind: a white female British rapper with both street cred and commercial success, both at home and across the pond in the U.S. Lady Sov (as she likes to be called) was raised on a cutthroat London council estate (housing project), where, inspired by her mother's Salt-N-Pepa records, she began writing songs when she was fourteen. She dropped out of high school shortly thereafter, and worked in a donut shop and cleaning windows while trying to make inroads in the hip-hop community by posting demos on the Internet. A male-versus-female MC battle she was involved in was released as a CD in 2003 and began to snowball interest in the tiny rapper with the outsize personality (at five-foot-one, she calls herself "the biggest midget in the game"), and before she knew it, she was being flown to New York to have a meeting with Jay-Z, who was so impressed by freestyle rhymes she whipped out for him in the Def Jam conference room that he signed her on the spot. Her subsequent debut album, *Public Warning*—a melange of grime, garage, hip-hop, dancehall, and punk, featuring collaborations with Missy Elliott—landed her a support slot on a Gwen Stefani tour in 2007, and set little Lady Sovereign on course to becoming huge.

LADY SOVEREIGN

SO I CAN'T DANCE AND I REALLY CAN'T SING /
I CAN ONLY DO ONE THING / AND THAT'S BE
LADY SOVEREIGN!— "LOVE ME OR HATE ME"

DOWNLOAD "Hoodie"

WEAR

adidas tracksuit
Sov's signature look is
a high side ponytail and
an adidas tracksuit (she
claims not to have worn a
skirt in over a decade). If
you squint, she resembles
Sporty Spice—but we know
who would win in a fight.

Georgia-born Charlyn Marie Marshall, a.k.a. Cat Power, has had an erratic and fraught, but stunning, career. Originally drawn to the art-rock scene upon moving to New York in 1992 (for one of her first performances, she played a two-string guitar and sang "no" over and over for twenty minutes), Marshall signed to Matador Records in 1996, but after releasing only one album she quit music altogether and moved to Oregon to work as a babysitter. While living in a farmhouse and suffering from nightmares, she began to write songs again, which were released as the critically lauded *Moon Pix* in 1998. Marshall possesses a plaintive, mournful, and haunting voice, which she offsets with skeletal arrangements and soft, sparse guitar accompaniment. A very fragile and notoriously intense performer, she's been known to stand with her back to the audience, or suddenly start screaming and leave the stage. However, in recent years she's become increasingly confident, and in addition to continuing to release stop-in-your-tracks gorgeous records, she's appeared in a film projected on the side of New York's Museum of Modern Art for a Doug Aitken exhibition in 2007 as well as in Wong Kar Wai's *Blueberry Nights*, and played for her friend Karl Lagerfeld at a Chanel couture show.

WHEN THEY PUT ME SIX FEET UNDERGROUND /
WILL THE BIG BAD BEAUTIFUL YOU BE AROUND?
— "THE MOON"

CAT POWER

PRIMP

Eyeliner pencil
True to her moniker, Marshall gives her eyes a feline look by lining the rims with black liner.

HEAR

The Covers Record (2000)
A covers album (the first of two) might seem an odd recommendation when her own material is so sublime, but trust us: Marshall breaks down the traditional vocal hooks of the original songs, stripping each to its essential, shiver-inducing core.

The Greatest (2006)
No, not a greatest hits record, but rather a magnificent collection of sweet, sun-kissed, southern country-soul songs that Marshall recorded in Memphis with many of the musicians Al Green had worked with in the '70s.

PLAY

Black Fender guitar
Marshall first picked up a guitar when she was nineteen. She still asserts that she never *really* learned to play—and that's a good thing.

DOWNLOAD "Lived in Bars"

PJ HARVEY

LICK MY LEGS / I'M ON FIRE
— "RID OF ME"

WEAR

Sparkly mini-dress
In the mid-'90s,
Harvey said that
her look was
"a combination
of being quite
elegant and funny
and revolting,
all at the same
time." But she
grew out of
the funny and
revolting part.

Rid of Me (1993)
An intense, tortured record epitomized by the title track, in which Harvey threatens what will happen if a lover leaves her. Producer Steve Albini later said she ate nothing but potatoes during the entire recording of the album.

Stories from the City, Stories from the Sea (2000)
The other side of Polly Jean: a joyous and emotionally open album, with sky-scraping guitars and life-affirming lyrics, inspired by a six-month stay in Manhattan in 1999.

White Chalk (2007)
An abrupt, stark departure for Miss Harvey, who for the first time laid her guitar aside to make this ghostly, delicate, piano-driven album. She's always been able to send shivers up spines, but on the sepulchral, spindly White Chalk, she does it in a totally new way.

Polly Jean Harvey cut a dynamic swathe through '90s alt-rock with her formidable, gutsy, blues spiked sound—compared to her, Britpop was a flash in the pan. Born in Somerset on October 9, 1969, and raised on a sheep farm in Dorset, Harvey studied saxophone for eight years and played in a number of local bands before she began writing her own songs at the age of eighteen. (Her first solo gig was so bad that the proprietor of the pub she was playing in begged her to stop lest he lose business.) Her 1992 debut album, the stark and powerful *Dry*, was recorded for under $5,000 and met with rapturous critical acclaim—and with every subsequent album both her image and her music has evolved. In the early days, her look was black turtlenecks, black leggings, and Doc Martens, but for her 1995 album *To Bring You My Love* (which spawned a major radio hit in the U.S., "Down By the Water," a song about drowning a baby), she adopted a more theatrical look—bright red lipstick, catsuits, and ball gowns—and by 2000's *Stories of the City, Stories from the Sea*, she had settled on a groomed, uptown glam look. Her lyrics explore mythology, sex, religion, love, and death, often with a sinister undercurrent, and Harvey is an intense, captivating performer who, despite having been in the spotlight for over a decade, has always maintained an air of mystery.

DOWNLOAD "The Mess We're In," a duet with Thom Yorke.

MEG WHITE

I DON'T CARE WHAT OTHER PEOPLE SAY /
I'M GOING TO LOVE YOU ANYWAY
— "IN THE COLD, COLD NIGHT"

HEAR

Elephant (2003)
Arguably the White Stripes'
greatest record, and the
one on which Meg moves out
from behind the drum kit and
takes her first stab at singing on the sweet, haunting
"In the Cold, Cold Night."

Get Behind Me Satan (2005)
On "Passive Manipulation,"
Meg's second-ever song,
she sings, "Women, listen
to your mothers / Don't
just succumb to the wishes
of your brothers / You
need to know the dif-
ference between a father
and a lover." Hmmm...

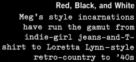

WEAR

Red, Black, and White
Meg's style incarnations
have run the gamut from
indie-girl jeans-and-T-
shirt to Loretta Lynn–style
retro-country to '40s
torch-singer glamour, but
of course she never strays
from red, black, and white.

WATCH

Under Blackpool Lights
(2004)
If you've never
seen the White
Stripes live, shame
on you. But until
you do, this is the
next best thing.

The White Stripes drummer is notoriously buttoned-up in interviews and keeps her biography carefully veiled, but the facts we do know are these: Meg White was born in Grosse Point, Michigan, in 1974, and met Jack (then Jack Gillis) while bartending at a Detroit bar. They were married on September 26, 1996 (he took her name), and, on a whim, she taught herself to drum along with some of the songs he was writing. They made their first public appearance as a band in July 1997 at a Detroit bar called the Gold Dollar, where they played two of their own composi- tions and a cover of "Love Potion Number 9." Although they divorced in 2000 and took to pass- ing themselves off as siblings, their musical partnership not only endured but also became the biggest thing to come out of the garage rock revival around the turn of the millennium. By 2001 they were headlining stadiums and turning a new generation on to the fading artistry of Delta blues. Onstage, Meg is a ponytailed cutie-pie with a sly grin, who never loses her cool or breaks a sweat, and although there has been criticism that her drumming is too basic, her minimalist but powerful style is the perfect complement to Jack's feats of derring-do on the guitar. Despite her notorious timidity, she has stepped forward to make a handful of notable appearances, namely modeling in ads for Marc Jacobs, and in Jim Jarmusch's 2003 film *Coffee and Cigarettes*.

DOWNLOAD "In the Cold, Cold Night"

THE KILLS

HEAR

No Wow (2005)
Eleven songs about obsessive love
and hate. Best listened to—at top
volume—when feeling angry.

IF I'M SO EVIL /
THEN WHY ARE YOU SATISFIED?
— "RODEO TOWN"

ALISON MOSSHART

With her face half obscured by a curtain of long
dark hair, an almost exclusively black wardrobe, and
a tendency to silently suck on cigarettes while her
bandmate Jamie Hince does most of the talking,
Alison Mosshart probably exudes cool through her
pores. She looks like she came straight out of 1960s
New York, but Mosshart grew up in the unlikely setting
of resort-town Vero Beach, Florida, where she started
her first punk band, Discount, at the age of fourteen.
It was while visiting London after Discount disbanded
that Mosshart met Hince—she was staying in the
apartment above him and used to hear him playing
guitar through the floorboards. When the pair formed
The Kills, they took on the names "VV" and "Hotel"
to signify a new beginning (the names haven't really
stuck), and started writing visceral, snarling, drum-
machine-assisted garage rock songs that owe a clear
debt to both Royal Trux and the Velvet Underground.
They recorded their sparse, stripped-down debut album, *Keep on Your Mean Side*, on vintage equipment
in London's ToeRag Studios (where the White Stripes
had just recorded *Elephant*) in 2002, and soon gained
notoriety for their kinetic live performances, in which
they appear to be locked in a taut, fraught confronta-
tion—Mosshart prowls the stage like a disturbed cat
while Hince slashes angrily at his guitar. Their 2005
major label debut, *No Wow*, garnered the duo even
more attention (and a lot of press speculation about
their relationship) and, although they ducked underground again for two years before emerging with its
follow up, *Midnight Boom*, it was worth the wait.

WEAR

Skinny black jeans
No one will
ever know how
dirty they are.

WATCH

"The Good Ones" Video
In which Mosshart and Hince perform as
the focal point of a Warhol-esque art
exhibition. Perfectly captures the almost
uncomfortably intense energy between them.

DOWNLOAD "Wait"

KAREN O

SHE WAS A PRIMAL INSTITUTION / SHE WAS A DANGER TO HERSELF — "MYSTERY GIRL"

PRIMP

Red lipstick
For when you've
got a date with
the night.

HEAR

Fever To Tell (2003)
The band's sonic dervish of a debut album. "Maps"—a ballad that can break hearts at one hundred paces—is worth the price of entry alone.

When the Yeah Yeah Yeahs first started creating a buzz on the New York music scene in 2000, the band's primal punk rock sound and unique structure (no bass!) were conversation starters, but Karen O was the selling point. A fearless performer who throws herself through the air, writhes on the floor, pours beer over her head, and practically gnaws on the microphone during particularly spirited shows, the raven-haired front woman (born Karen Orzolek in 1978) is riveting to behold, and it's no surprise she has made going from downtown party girl to international art-rock superstar look like a snap. Dressed in outrageous, colorful get-ups (most of them devised by her fashion-designer friend Christian Joy), and blessed with a voice that swoops from glass-shattering Poly Styrene–esque screams to sweet crooning sighs, Karen telegraphs both an edgy eroticism and a charmingly goofy elegance. The band's music—a party-mix-ready romp from the galloping racket of songs such as "Date with the Night" to the glam stomp of "Gold Lion" to tender, softly sung slow-jams like "Modern Romance"—is fun and cathartic, and Karen O embodies the band's ethos of strength and individuality; hedonism with heart.

Yeah Yeah Yeahs EP (2005)
The YYY's incendiary first EP is hard to top. "Bang" slipped past radio censors before anyone figured out that Karen was singing, "As a fuck, son, you suck."

WEAR

Fingerless gloves
The signature Karen O accessory.

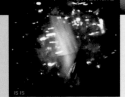

WATCH

Is Is (2007)
The DVD accompanying the *Is Is* EP was shot with a night-vision camera during a YYY's show at Brooklyn's Glasslands Gallery, where the band did two sets—one for everyone, and a second, Riot Grrrl style, just for the ladies.

DOWNLOAD "Black Tongue"

JOANNA NEWSOM

AND EVERYTHING WITH WINGS IS RESTLESS,
AIMLESS, DRUNK AND DOUR / THE BUTTERFLIES
AND BIRDS COLLIDE AT HOT, UNGODLY HOURS
— "EMILY"

HEAR

Ys (2006)
With orchestral arrange-
ments by Van Dyke Parks
and production from Steve
Albini, *Ys* is a rich
tapestry of a record,
complete with fantasy-and
allegory-laced lyrics,
intricately plangent
melodies, and what might
be the first use of the
expression chim-choo-ree
on a rock record ever.

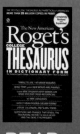

READ

Thesaurus
So that you, too, can someday
pen lines like: "With hydro-
cephalitic listlessness ants mop
up-a their brow" ("Emily").

WEAR

Fur hat
Newsom's whimsical fashion
sense is as inspiringly out-
there as her music. The girl
wore a wolf pelt on her head
in the promo pics for *Ys*, and
still looked good.

A virtuoso harp player with the woodland-sprite looks of a *Dark Crystal* Gelfling, Joanna Newsom has made her mark as one of the most peculiar and beguiling artists in today's indie-rock realm. Born in 1982 in Nevada City, California, she began to study Celtic harp at the age of seven. Later, while studying at Mills College, she formed a post-punk band called the Pleased along with three musician friends. They released one album in 2003 before she went solo and began to hone her distinctive fusion of Appalachian folk, African kora, avant-garde orchestration, and lyrics that read like medieval verse. She signed to Drag City and released her somewhat polarizing debut album, *The Milk-Eyed Mender*, in 2004, which was followed in 2006 by the ambitiously conceived *Ys*. With her swooping, yowling, breathily Björk-esque singing voice and knack for poetic turns of phrase, Newsom has been called freak-folk, psych-folk, and countless variations thereof. Whatever it is, she's definitely doing her own thing, and for that, we salute her.

DOWNLOAD "Monkey & Bear"

LILY ALLEN

HEAR

Alright, Still (2007)
With happy, ska-tinged beats and sassy lyrics, Allen blasts hypocrisy, taking on everyone from ex-boyfriends to club bouncers.

The daughter of British comedian Keith Allen (who appeared, memorably, in Blur's "Country House" video), Lily is endowed with a wicked wit and a quick tongue, and a talent for penning cheeky, undeniably catchy, zeitgeist-capturing songs. Her adolescence was rocky—she attended thirteen schools, and was expelled from several—and she worked as a florist and at a record store in Ibiza before her songs caught fire on the Internet: She posted demos on MySpace, along with an opinionated, gossipy blog, which caused a commotion that prompted EMI Records to rush-release her debut album, *Alright, Still*, in 2006 (it hit American shores in 2007). Produced by man-with-the-golden-touch Mark Ronson, the record sets Allen's observational, often scathing lyrics to exuberant, skipping-in-the-sun melodies and showcases her sweet, Cockney-inflected singing voice. It's little surprise that it proved to be an international success, or that Allen's downtown-cool fashion style (characterized by cute vintage frocks worn with kicks, high ponytails, and winged fluorescent eyeliner), lighthearted videos (like that for "Smile," in which she spikes an ex-boyfriend's coffee with laxatives) and bawdy, smoking, drinking, swearing, straight-talking persona have already made her a bona fide modern-day icon.

WEAR

Knocker earrings
Allen is a major earring junkie, and pairs like these are her favorites.

DOWNLOAD "Not Big"

Kala (2007)
M.I.A.'s second album
will scramble your
brain—in the best
way imaginable.

Arular (2005)
M.I.A.'s mighty debut
is a melange of
genres, unleashed at
breakneck speed and
delivered with her
characteristic moxie.
Totally original.

M.I.A.

SLANG TANG, THAT'S THE M.I.A. THANG /
I GOT THE BOMBS TO MAKE YOU BLOW /
I GOT THE BEATS TO MAKE IT BANG
— "PULL UP THE PEOPLE"

A sort of Technicolor global cheerleader for the twenty-first century, M.I.A. was born Maya Arulpragasam in London in 1977, the daughter of a Sri Lankan Tamil activist. She was a graffiti artist before turning to music—a similarly lawless, mix-and-match sensibility shines through everything she does—and she's touched down pretty much everywhere in the world, collecting influences that fuel her fearless, rapid-fire musical melange of electro, hip-hop, grime, tribal rhythms, and pop. Her 2005 debut album, *Arular* (named after her father), was a politically charged tour de force, and its success landed her a guest appearance on Missy Elliott's *Cookbook* album and the support slot on Gwen Stefani's Harajuku Lovers world tour. Her jarring, uncompromising, in-your-face 2007 follow-up, *Kala* (named after her mother), placed the singer even more firmly on the front line of musical innovation with its disjointed beats (provided on one track by thirty Indian drummers) and colorful, smart wordplay. Even if it sometimes sounds like she's singing gibberish, with M.I.A., you can be sure there's always a message in there somewhere.

DOWNLOAD "Paper Planes"

PRIMP

Green or yellow nail polish
Even her fingernails
are subversive.

WATCH

"Bird Flu" Video
Filming on loca-
tion on the
southern coast
of India, M.I.A.
recruited a bunch
of funky-dancing
locals—and a cou-
ple of chickens—
for this video.

WEAR

Tie-dye pants
If anyone
can bring
tie-dye back,
it's M.I.A.

AMY WINEHOUSE

HEAR

Back to Black (2007)
Frank is spectacular, too, but this is the record you'll still be playing when you're eighty.

They tried to make her go to rehab, but she said "no, no, no"—and instead made one of the biggest records of 2007, *Back to Black*. A hard-drinking, heavily-tattooed Jewish girl from London who sings like Nina Simone and wears her hair in a gigantic beehive like a dirty Ronnie Spector, Amy Winehouse may make music your parents would love, but you'd never bring her home to meet them. Her début album, the R&B- and jazz-inflected *Frank*, was released in 2003 and though "Stronger Than Me" won the prestigious Ivor Novello Award, the album failed to make much of a commercial splash. However, its follow-up, *Back to Black*, a tormented record about cheating, breaking up, getting wasted, and getting back together again, was a stroke of genius: With the help of producer Mark Ronson, Winehouse was able to set her raw, often ribald, lyrics against a magnificent Motown-esque musical backdrop. The next thing she knew, *Spin* and *Rolling Stone* were fighting over who would get her on a cover first, *Us Weekly* was photographing her taking out the garbage, "Rehab" had become the "Crazy" of 2007, and she was drawing rapturous crowds everywhere she went. In typical Winehouse fashion, though, she merely shrugs it off, saying, "I'm not in this to be a role model." Yet in offering an alternative to the depthless, plastic pop that her songs have shunted down the charts, she has become just that—well, barring the substance-abuse problem.

PRIMP

Black eyeliner
For that perfect winged-out line. Steady hands not required.

Lush Rehab shampoo
She might not have wanted to go, go, go, but her hair sure needs it.

DOWNLOAD "Tears Dry On Their Own"

IN THE END NO ONE'S INNOCENT /
BIG OR SMALL IT MAKES NO DIFFERENCE /
GET UP, STAND OUT, AND HOLD YOUR HEAD UP
HIGHER, HIGHER — "FIRE WITH FIRE"

BETH DITTO

WATCH

"Jealous Girls" on YouTube
The Gossip's videos are
Day-Glo explosions of
'80s graphics and some
serious boogying.

HEAR

Standing in the Way of Control (2006)
Blues and soul-inflected
disco-punk like nobody's
ever done it before.
With songs that rail against
the breakdown of civil
rights and rally for girl
power, this is a megawatt
album with a message.

WEAR

Vintage frock
Ditto tears down
stereotypes about
what lesbian women
should look like
and what larger
women should
wear. If she
wants to don gold
lamé catsuits,
belts with patent
leather bows, and
lashings of eye
shadow, goddammit
she's going to do
it. Her best look
to copy: suit-
ably loud, retro
polka-dot dresses
like this one.

Beth Ditto was declared the "coolest person in rock" by a 2006 *NME* magazine poll—she famously went on to pose nude for the magazine's cover the following summer—and it's still hard to debate that title. Born in 1981 in squirrel-eatingly rural Searcy, Arkansas, Ditto grew up as a proud lesbian punk rocker in the heart of the Bible Belt. In 1999, heavily influenced by the feminist politics of the Riot Grrrl scene, she started The Gossip with Brace Paine and Kathy Mendonca (later replaced by Hannah Blilie) and moved to Olympia, Washington. Seven years, three albums, and three EPs later, the band finally won big-time acclaim in the U.K., thanks in part to *NME*'s support. Their electrifying 2006 album, *Standing in the Way of Control*, slapped the British mainstream on its ass and landed the formidable Ditto on the cover of just about every music magazine across the pond, despite the fact that much of the album's subject matter was distinctly American: the title song was written as a protest to George Bush's stance on gay marriage. With her hollering, gospel-tinged singing voice, outlandish stage getups (think metallic Cleopatra headdresses, tiger-print leotards, bikinis, and stilettos), and defiantly maverick attitude, Ditto is certainly hard to miss. She flouts convention at every turn—whether it's embracing (and literally exposing) her, uh, above-average-pop-tart-physique (famously, she refused to play at über-hip London fashion emporium Topshop because they didn't stock her size) or her indefatigable support for gay rights—yet never fails to be brazenly honest and inspirational (qualities she has put to use as a regular advice columnist for the U.K.'s *Guardian*), all while turning out some of the best dance floor–filling disco anthems of the decade.

DOWNLOAD The Le Tigre remix of "Standing in the Way of Control."

AND FROM ANY SOURCE IMAGINABLE—
NO ONE WORKS (OR PLAYS) IN A
VACUUM—AND IT CAN MANIFEST
ITSELF IN ANYTHING, FROM THE WAY
SOMEONE DRESSES TO THE WAY HE OR
SHE HOLDS A MICROPHONE. SO WHO—
OR WHAT—IS INFLUENCING THE
PEOPLE WHO ARE MAKING THE MUSIC
THAT IS CURRENTLY INFLUENCING US?
WE TALKED TO SOME OF THEM TO FIND
OUT, AND WHAT WE DISCOVERED WAS
ALWAYS INTERESTING, SOMETIMES
TRULY SURPRISING (THE SPICE GIRLS
WERE MENTIONED—MORE THAN
ONCE!), AND MAY CHANGE THE WAY YOU
LISTEN TO THEIR SONGS—AND THE
SONGS OF OTHERS—FROM NOW ON.

CHAPTER **2**

ENCES

THE DONNAS

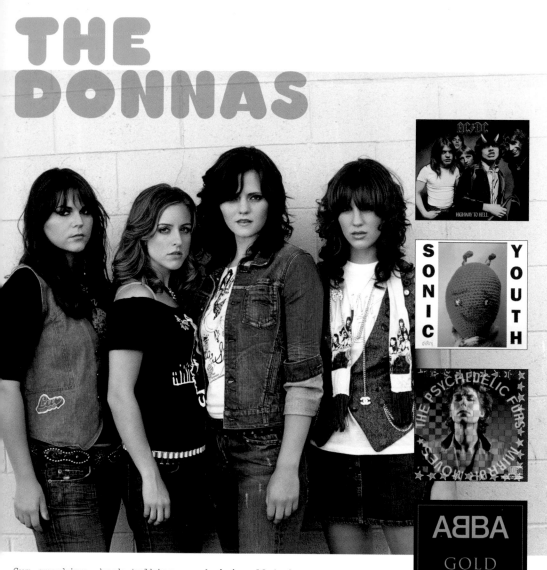

Gum-smacking, back-talking, rock 'n' roll bad-girls The Donnas have been playing together since eighth grade, and while they have many stories from when they started out about putting up with "girls can't play" accusations, they've more than proven themselves with seven albums of awesomeness. Here, singer Brett Anderson, guitarist Allison Robertson, bass player Maya Ford, and drummer Torry Castellano tag-team to tell us what turns them on and what they love to turn up.

Britney Spears

Ratt

Wendy O. Williams

WHO OR WHAT FIRST MADE YOU WANT TO MAKE MUSIC?

Brett: Listening to the radio in my bedroom and taping my own "show" on a cassette.

NAME FIVE ALBUMS THAT HAVE BEEN MOST INFLUENTIAL FOR YOU.

Brett: AC/DC, _Highway to Hell_; L7, _Bricks Are Heavy_; Mötley Crüe, _Too Fast For Love_; Sonic Youth, _Dirty_; Supergrass, _I Should Coco_.

FIRST RECORD YOU EVER OWNED?

Brett: A Jimmy Buffett "Margaritaville" 7-inch.

FIRST CONCERT?

Brett: Salt-n-Pepa at the Ohio State Fair.

DESCRIBE THE FEELING OF BEING ONSTAGE.

Brett: Adrenaline!! Better than a thousand cups of coffee!!

WHAT INSTRUMENTS DO YOU PLAY AND HOW DID YOU LEARN?

Allison: I play guitar mostly. I dabble in other things like keys, but guitar is number one. I learned by playing along to R.E.M. records, Kiss, Sonic Youth, Mötley Crüe, and surf songs. I taught myself by picking out the melodies, and I still do that now. I practice guitar more effectively by listening to music than by playing it with my fingers.

WHO ARE YOUR STYLE ICONS?

Allison: My style icons are Wendy O. Williams, David Lee Roth, Stevie Nicks, Siouxsie Sioux, and Stephen Pearcy of Ratt.

WHAT BAND THAT YOU NEVER GOT TO SEE PERFORM WOULD YOU LOVE TO SEE?

Allison: Girlschool with Kelly Johnson, and ABBA!

IF YOU COULD COLLABORATE WITH ANYONE, WHO WOULD IT BE?

Allison: M.I.A. and/or Glenn Danzig.

WHAT'S THE FIRST RECORD YOU REACH FOR WHEN YOU NEED TO BE CHEERED UP?

Maya: Psychedelic Furs, _Mirror Moves_. It's always in my car.

WHAT'S THE FIRST RECORD YOU REACH FOR WHEN YOU WOULD RATHER NOT BE CHEERED UP?

Maya: ABBA, _Gold_. I listen to that and cry when I get dumped.

WHO IS THE MOST UNDERAPPRECIATED ARTIST IN YOUR OPINION?

Maya: Ratt!

WHAT'S THE BEST CONCERT YOU'VE EVER BEEN TO?

Maya: Britney Spears in Vegas at the MGM Grand. O-Town opened and I got to go on stage and dance with them. I held [Trevor Penick's] hand. He's my favorite. He sang some stupid love song to me. Then I got on the piano and pretended to be enraptured while Ashley [Parker Angel] did a solo. When I walked back to my seat all the twelve-year-old girls in the crowd were cursing me. Britney was awesome. It rained onstage and she did somersaults in a cowboy hat.

WHAT ARE YOUR BIGGEST NONMUSICAL INFLUENCES?

Torry: When we're in the process of writing, I would say that my dreams are a big influence on the music. I like to read, watch movies, look at photographs, even look at certain clothes, and then when I go to sleep I think that my subconscious scrambles it all in my dreams, so when I wake up I usually have some new ideas, or a new direction. Also, a good, long night out can help with content!

WHAT DID YOU LISTEN TO AS A TEENAGER AND HOW HAS IT AFFECTED THE MUSIC YOU MAKE?

Torry: I loved metal when I was a teenager; it has always stayed with me. I always try to bring some of that harder edge to our music. Even though it's not thought of as catchy music, I also think that there are a lot of hooks in metal that can be very inspiring. And, of course, head-banging is the best!

WHAT'S YOUR FAVORITE MUSIC VIDEO?

Torry: I love the video for "Hot for Teacher" by Van Halen. I love how they use black-and-white for some of the shots and then when the girls get on the desks and dance, it's all in color. It's funny and abstract without being cartoony. Even though I've seen it many times, I always watch the whole thing when it's on.

WHAT'S YOUR ADVICE FOR PEOPLE WANTING TO START BANDS?

Torry: I believe that anyone can pick up an instrument and start a band, but no matter how much raw talent you have, you can always improve. Challenge yourself!

TAHITA BULMER

NEW YOUNG PONY CLUB

Since they formed in 2004, five-piece
New Wave/New Rave electronica band
New Young Pony Club have been making
people hit the dance floor with their
quirky party anthems and high-en-
ergy live shows, at which flamboyant
frontwoman Tahita Bulmer is front and
center. She and the band graduated
from local cult favorite in their
hometown of London to the ranks of
international rock stars when they
signed with Australian label Modular
and produced their breakout, Mercury
Prize-nominated debut album, *Fantastic Playroom*, which was released in
the U.S. in 2007.

WHAT RECORDS HAVE BEEN MOST SIGNIFICANT TO YOU?

The Stooges, *Fun House*;
Public Enemy, *Fear of a Black Planet*;
Blur, *Modern Life is Rubbish*;
Portishead, *Dummy*;
LCD Soundsystem, "Losing My Edge."

WHAT WAS YOUR FIRST CONCERT?

Blur. Perhaps somewhat predictably. But they were really cute and far cooler than bloody Take That, which is what all my school friends were into.

WHAT MUSIC DID YOU LISTEN TO AS A TEENAGER AND HOW HAS IT AFFECTED THE MUSIC YOU MAKE NOW?

I listened to a lot of rap and hip-hop plus indie like the Stone Roses, Blur, and Radiohead, and old punk and post-punk bands like Blondie and Television. It's all definitely influenced the music I make now, particularly the post-punk sound and the lyrical dexterity of the old-school rap fraternity.

WHO ARE YOUR STYLE ICONS?

Sort of a mish-mash of '40s, '50s, and '70s disco style. Debbie Harry, Ava Gardner, Rita Hayworth, Katharine Hepburn, Bettie Page, and Stella Starr and all those groupie girls that you see in pictures of David Bowie, Iggy Pop, and CBGB in the late '70s.

WHEN YOU THINK OF AN AMAZING LIVE PERFORMER, WHO COMES TO MIND?

David Bowie, Madonna, Prince, Iggy Pop, Lovefoxx, Mick Jagger, Mark E. Smith, Ana Matronic, and Jake Shears. All of them are very different. Some very natural, others obviously performing through super-theatrical alter egos.

WHO HAS BEEN MOST INFLUENTIAL FOR YOU?

I think Madonna has been an influence on every female performer born in the past thirty years. Iggy, definitely. I am quite theatrical though. I could never be as natural as Lovefoxx appears. I'm far too introverted.

WHAT INSTRUMENTS DO YOU PLAY AND HOW DID YOU LEARN?

None. I've tried them all and I can't play anything properly. I can sing a melody line for someone else to play, though. All you really need is a good ear for music.

IF YOU COULD COLLABORATE WITH ANYONE, WHO WOULD IT BE?

Timbaland or Pharrell Williams, of course.

WHAT RECORD ALWAYS MAKES YOU WANT TO DANCE?

"Crazy in Love." Also "Town Called Malice" by the Jam.

WHAT RECORD DO YOU REACH FOR WHEN YOU'RE FEELING ANGRY?

"Fight the Power"—or any Public Enemy.

WHAT ARE YOUR BIGGEST NONMUSICAL INFLUENCES?

Films, books, fashion. I think it's impossible not to be influenced by what is around you.

DESCRIBE THE FEELING OF BEING ONSTAGE.

Terrifying, exhilarating, orgasmic, disappointing, energizing. There is nothing like it. Even during the most amazing gigs, you have moments where the audience is losing it and the band is too, when you think "what the fuck am I doing?" It's different every time.

Ava Gardner

Bettie Page

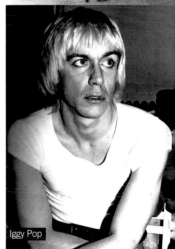

Iggy Pop

The Scissor Sisters

Rita Hayworth

JENNY LEWIS

RILO KILEY

Former child star Jenny Lewis (Troop Beverly Hills) formed Rilo Kiley with then-boyfriend Blake Sennett in 1998. Their music has evolved from the amped-up indie rock of their 2001 debut, Take Offs and Landings, to the sassy, classy, sophisticated soul-and-disco sound of 2007's Under the Blacklight. Meanwhile Lewis's 2006 solo album, Rabbit Fur Coat, saw her indulging her love of country and gospel—with wonderful, heart-stirring results. That she can comfortably (and successfully) dabble in a range of musical genres is one of the things we like best about her—and that she's probably the only person to have both guest-starred on Baywatch and opened for Coldplay.

The Carpenters

Pavement

WHAT FIRST SPARKED YOUR DESIRE TO MAKE MUSIC?

My parents are both musicians, so music was a huge part of my childhood. They had a lounge act in Las Vegas in the '70s called "Love's Way." My dad is a virtuosic harmonica player. He was a little young for vaudeville but he joined up with a group called the Harmonicats when he was twelve or thirteen. He put a harmonica in my crib (I threw it out), and we were always singing together. I started writing my first songs when I was about ten, and I remember the first folk song I wrote with one of my best friends when I was thirteen; it was called "You Can't Trust the Men of Today"…I haven't changed very much.

WHAT DID YOU LISTEN TO AS A TEENAGER AND HOW DID THAT AFFECT YOU LATER?

We all start out at the mercy of our parents' musical taste but luckily my mother had a great record collection, and I started out listening to Lou Reed, Karen Carpenter, and Barbara Streisand. But when I was old enough, I wanted to rebel against the music that she liked, so I started listening to hip-hop when I was about twelve, and listened to it exclusively for a couple years. Then I discovered Pavement and Built to Spill, and that changed me drastically. While I was listening to hip-hop I was writing poems, but when I started listening to rock music I picked up a guitar.

DID YOU TEACH YOURSELF HOW TO PLAY GUITAR?

I got a guitar for Christmas when I was fifteen. I asked for an acoustic and my mom bought me an electric. She had a boyfriend at the time who knew a couple chords and he taught me how

to play "Desperado." The first twenty songs that I wrote had those chords but with different words.

WHAT THREE RECORDS HAVE HAD THE GREATEST IMPACT ON YOU AND WHY?

The first time I fell in love with background vocals was listening to Lou Reed's _Transformer_. Now, the first thing that I hear after I have written a song is the background. De La Soul's _Three Feet High and Rising_ sonically blew me away. I still hear songs that were sampled on that record and think, "Oh my God, the first time I heard that was on _Three Feet High and Rising_! And Built to Spill, _There's Nothing Wrong With Love_. I heard that in the early days of Rilo Kiley and it just made an incredible impression on me.

WHAT WAS THE FIRST CONCERT YOU EVER WENT TO?

A Joe Cocker concert that I went to with my mom, but I don't really count that one. She was screaming, "I love you, Joe! I love you, Joe!" and I was so embarrassed I had to wait out in the lobby. My first concert without my mother was The Cure, the Pixies, and Love and Rockets at Dodger Stadium.

IN WHAT ENVIRONMENT OR STATE OF MIND DO YOU DO YOUR BEST WRITING?

My living room in the morning. I wake up most days at 8:36 a.m. It's really unnerving. I open my eyes and there's the clock and it's 8:36. On better days I wake up in the 9s, have a cup or two of coffee, and get to work.

IF THERE IS ANYONE YOU COULD COLLABORATE WITH, LIVING OR DEAD, WHO WOULD IT BE?

Laura Nyro. But she's dead, sadly.

LOUISE BASILIEN
PLASTISCINES

Plasticines are proof positive that girls do just want to have fun. Three teenagers from the Parisian suburbs, bassist Louise Basilien, singer/guitarist Katty Besnard, and guitarist Marine Neuilly met when they were still in high school and quickly set about writing songs and teaching themselves to play instruments. Singing in both French and English, Plastiscines' songs are energetic bursts that reflect a mix of influences both new and old. Though they were far from drinking age when they released their 2007 debut album, *LP1*, the girls love classic punk bands like Blondie and the Ramones, and as they were weaned on the Strokes, the White Stripes, and the Libertines, the resulting mix certainly does let the good times roll.

WHAT MADE YOU WANT TO START A BAND?

We all always loved rock 'n' roll, and when we were around fifteen or sixteen years old the only thing we could do was go to gigs. So when we saw those bands on stage, we said, "Oh that's what we want to do, we want to be on stage and play music and tour and stuff."

WHAT BANDS WERE YOU SEEING AT THAT POINT?

I think one of the gigs that really gave us the will to do music was the Strokes performing with Kings of Leon and Ben Kweller two years ago. That was the moment we said, "We really want to have a band."

WHAT MUSIC WERE YOU INTO GROWING UP?

Mostly '60s and '70s rock, like the B-52's, Blondie, the Ramones, and the Stooges—that's our background.

CAN YOU NAME ANY PARTICULARLY INFLUENTIAL ALBUMS?

That's too hard a question! Maybe *Plastic Letters* from Blondie…but I could never narrow it down.

The B-52's

DID YOU HAVE A MUSICAL BACK-GROUND?

No. We didn't go to music school, we just taught ourselves how to play guitar and the bass…and just played on. It was good that we learned at the same time because we progressed together.

WHAT WAS THE FIRST RECORD THAT YOU EVER BOUGHT?

One of the first albums I had when I was about eight years old was a Spice Girls! I think, for me, the first record I bought, which means the first rock 'n' roll album I bought, was *White Blood Cells* by the White Stripes.

WHAT WAS YOUR FIRST CONCERT?

I think it was the Libertines in 2004, though I went to see Eels with my dad when I was ten years old. But for Katty and Marine, it was the Strokes' first concert in Paris.

DO YOU HAVE A FAVORITE MUSIC VIDEO OR MOVIE OR DOCUMENTARY?

I love *24 Hour Party People*. It's just a really, really good music movie.

IF YOU COULD COLLABORATE WITH OR PLAY WITH ANYONE, WHO WOULD IT BE?

The Kings of Leon because we've really liked them for such a long time—we love their music.

WHO ARE YOUR FASHION ICONS?

Definitely Debbie Harry and Patti Smith. They are such amazing female rock 'n' roll icons. They have such great style and a special feeling about them.

WHEN YOU WRITE SONGS WHAT ARE YOUR MAIN INSPIRATIONS?

We're just nineteen-year-old girls, so we talk a lot about boys and relationships and everyday life. It's all very simple, not too dark, but quite fun.

WHAT ADVICE DO YOU HAVE FOR PEOPLE WANTING TO START BANDS?

Just have fun with friends. That is the most important thing. Just enjoy music and life, always.

WHAT DOES IT FEEL LIKE TO BE ONSTAGE?

It's great! Hard to explain, but just amazing. After one song you just don't want to leave the stage.

Debbie Harry with Blondie   Patti Smith   The Ramones

JULIETTE LEWIS

When Oscar-nominated actress Juliette Lewis took a break from the big screen to start a band, Juliette and the Licks, in 2003, it was a ballsy move, but one that the group's two visceral, supercharged albums (*You're Speaking My Language* and *Four on the Floor*) and rocktastic live shows have more than justified. She's a fearless, slightly unhinged performer who patently doesn't care what anyone thinks—and her passion for music is admirably boundless.

WHO OR WHAT INITIALLY MADE YOU WANT TO DO MUSIC?

The first performer who made me go, "What the—? That's awesome!" was David Lee Roth in the Van Halen "Panama" video. I think I was like thirteen when I first saw it. There's a moment when he calls to the camera and, I was like, "I want to do *that*." I loved his showmanship, his playful energy, and his pure sex appeal… And I liked his pants.

NAME THE SONGS THAT HAVE HAD THE BIGGEST INFLUENCE ON YOU.

Jimi Hendrix, "Voodoo Child (Slight Return)." I often use music when I'm acting, to prepare for scenes or evoke feelings, and this was a song I listened to a lot while making *Natural Born Killers*. To me, it represented danger, chaos, beauty, and hunger.

Nina Simone, "Nobody Loves You When You're Down and Out." This is a song I like to cover and sing a capella from time to time. It really speaks to me. It's an old

time song—bluesy, with piano— and it's this whole story of hard times and triumphs.

Patti Smith, "Rock 'n' Roll Nigger." What an integral part of my life! Oliver Stone turned me on to Patti Smith when he used this song in the sound track for *Natural Born Killers*. It's radical: She's taking that word and making it something powerful for all of us. It's about being a rock 'n' roll outsider, and being the underdog. I love it.

PJ Harvey, "Hardly Wait." When I discovered PJ Harvey a long time ago, I loved the drama in her singing. It's inspired me a lot vocally, because it's not about technical perfection, it's about emotion. All of her stuff is so sexy and dangerous—when she first came out, there was nothing like her, and there's still nothing like her today. But I also have to mention Janis Joplin, "Ball and Chain," because it's an incredible, dark rock 'n' roll song that I listened to incessantly when I was fifteen.

David Lee Roth

The Rocky Horror Picture Show

Nina Simone

The Jimi Hendrix Experience

WHAT WAS THE FIRST CONCERT YOU EVER WENT TO?

You're going to laugh. LL Cool J, in San Francisco. I went through a whole rap phase when I was thirteen, which was quite rebellious at the time because it was before hip-hop went mainstream. Being in love with black boys and listening to early rap was pretty radical. But then my first rock show was Nirvana, around 1993. It was such a powerful experience to see a front man completely own the audience like that. Kurt Cobain was famously introverted and melancholy, but he was so far reaching.

WHAT DID YOU LISTEN TO AS A TEENAGER AND HOW DID IT AFFECT WHAT YOU DO NOW?

After my rap phase, I got into the Cure and Depeche Mode, and then I went into my '60s phase. So when everyone else was listening to Pearl Jam and Nirvana, I was listening to Hendrix and the Beatles and Janis Joplin.

WHO ARE YOUR STYLE ICONS?

I don't model myself off of anyone, but there are certain people I like visually. Blondie had a great dirty-glam look. I like avant-garde people like Grace Jones and Karen O, but I also like things that are accessible—I'm not into corseted, polished, restrictive looks. I'm also attracted to dancers and circus performers. On the bus, I tend to wear my white Diesel jeans and my old red boots and whatever I pick up on the road.

IF YOU COULD COLLABORATE WITH ANYONE, LIVING OR DEAD, WHO WOULD IT BE?

Jimi Hendrix had such a cooking band, I'd like to play with them.

WHAT BAND THAT YOU NEVER GOT TO SEE PLAY WOULD YOU LIKE TO HAVE SEEN?

James Brown. I really missed out, because he's gone now, and I could have seen him a couple of years ago. And all of those '60s bands like Led Zeppelin and Janis Joplin…I probably wouldn't have lived very well back then.

WHAT RECORD ALWAYS CHEERS YOU UP?

I've got two! [*Endless Summer:*] *Donna Summer's Greatest Hits*. We do the most rocking, fun cover of "Hot Stuff," and we've played it everywhere from Spain to Finland to Turkey, and it's a crowd-pleaser through and through.

And secondly, Bachman Turner Overdrive, "Taking Care of Business." I swear if you put that song on in the morning when you wake up, you'll feel motivated all day. Try that: Put it on when you're brushing your teeth.

WHAT SONGS ALWAYS MAKE YOU FEEL SAD?

There's a John Lee Hooker song called "My Dream," and it's *so fucking sad!* He sees a mirage of love he knew that was no longer there…such a beautiful song, and really simple. And there's a Foo Fighters song called "Exhausted." It's draining, and there's pain in it… it's great.

WHAT IS YOUR FAVORITE MUSIC VIDEO, MOVIE, OR DOCUMENTARY?

Oh my god, *The Rocky Horror Picture Show*! It's my number one favorite. I first saw it when I was ten, and it was a *huge* influence on me. I got to shoot pictures with Mick Rock not long ago—the legendary photographer who shot Blondie and Bowie and Iggy—and he had shot all of the promotional stills that were used for *Rocky Horror Picture Show*, so he gave me a book and I was *so* excited. As far as documentaries go, [the D.A. Pennebaker] Bob Dylan documentary, *Don't Look Back*, is classic.

DESCRIBE THE FEELING OF BEING ONSTAGE.

When all of the rock 'n' roll planets align, it's like every cell is open and every muscle is worked and warm and flexed, and there's a swirling of energy in the room. It's totally transcendent, and there's an immense sense of unity. You get all of these people in a room from different walks of life, different cultures, and you come together. When everything is at its best, it's like moving through a hurricane, it's that visceral.

WHAT WOULD YOUR ADVICE BE TO PEOPLE WHO WANT TO START BANDS?

You've got to be in it to win it. You've got to be willing to work your ass off, and you've got to want to give, not just take. And do it independently all the way. In our group, it's been total DIY. We've never had a major label involved—it begins and ends with the live show. You've got to find your audience and then grow your audience. That's your quest.

ELEANOR FRIEDBERGER

THE FIERY FURNACES

As half of Brooklyn-based duo The Fiery Furnaces (her brother Matt makes up the other half), Eleanor Friedberger has become a very recognizable figure on the indie-rock circuit—while somehow also managing to maintain an air of mystery. Her effortlessly cool stage demeanor and inimitable way of singing the band's quirky, hyper-literate lyrics telegraph a brainy insouciance, and it's little surprise that she has become an inspiration for fashion-folk and fans alike (not to mention her boyfriend, Alex Kapranos of Franz Ferdinand, who wrote his band's song "Eleanor Put Your Boots Back On" just for her).

149

WHO OR WHAT FIRST MADE YOU WANT TO MAKE MUSIC?

Gary Busey's performance in *The Buddy Holly Story*.

WHAT ALBUMS OR SONGS HAVE BEEN MOST INFLUENTIAL FOR YOU?

Led Zeppelin's *Physical Graffiti*, Van Morrison's *Astral Weeks*, and Jorge Ben's *A Tábua de Esmeralda*.

WHAT WAS THE FIRST RECORD YOU EVER OWNED?

Most likely the Broadway cast recording of *Annie* or *The Chipmunks a Go-Go*. Soon followed by Cabbage Patch Kids' *Cabbage Patch Dreams* and the sound track to *The Muppets Take Manhattan*. One of the first records I actually bought myself was the sound track to *Stand By Me* in 1986.

FIRST CONCERT?

Robert Plant, Rosemont Horizon. A concert promoter rep spotted us thirteen-year-old girls in the nosebleed seats, wearing our new Robert Plant T-shirts. Magically, he led us down to second-row center seats and said, "Enjoy the show."

WHAT INSTRUMENTS DO YOU PLAY AND HOW DID YOU LEARN?

The Korg KAOSS Pad; [I learned] by pointing my finger at people.

WHO ARE YOUR STYLE ICONS?

My great-aunts, Boula and Mary.

WHAT ARTIST OR BAND WHOM YOU NEVER GOT TO SEE PERFORM WOULD YOU LOVE TO SEE?

Bob Dylan with the Band, Bo Diddley, Nina Simone, the Ramones, Captain Beefheart, the Velvet Underground, the Replacements, Howlin' Wolf, Aretha Franklin, The Who, Johnny Cash, the Clash, Caetano Veloso, Ike and Tina Turner…

IF YOU COULD COLLABORATE WITH ANYONE, WHO WOULD IT BE?

My brother, and only my brother!

FIRST RECORD YOU REACH FOR WHEN YOU NEED TO BE CHEERED UP?

Ethiopiques, Volume 3. It's a collection featuring Ethiopian singers and musicians.

FIRST RECORD YOU REACH FOR WHEN YOU WOULD RATHER NOT BE CHEERED UP?

Anything sung by Ronnie Lane.

MOST OVERLOOKED ARTIST OR RECORD IN YOUR OPINION?

Richard Davies's solo albums and especially his record as The Moles, *Instinct*.

BEST CONCERT YOU'VE EVER BEEN TO?

The Jesus Lizard at Emo's, Austin, Texas, 1994.

BIGGEST NONMUSICAL INFLUENCES?

Walter Payton, *Danny, the Champion of the World*, Carlton Fisk, Woody Allen, *The Wire*, Sydney Pollack, Donald Sutherland, Greek cooking, Old English sheepdogs, Roman Meal bread, *Mean Streets*, Little League softball coaches, the "Cinderella" attraction at Disney World, large thrift stores arranged by color, Julia Child, Terence Conran's *The House Book* from 1974…I could go on and on.

FAVORITE MUSIC MOVIE, VIDEO, OR DOCUMENTARY?

The Sound of Music and *The Kids Are Alright*.

ANY ADVICE FOR PEOPLE WANTING TO START BANDS?

Practice three to six hours a day.

WHAT DID YOU LISTEN TO AS A TEENAGER AND HOW HAS IT AFFECTED THE MUSIC YOU MAKE?

Chicago's Oldies 104.3 and WCKG Classic Rock 105.9; [these stations] made me want to be in a really good band…as opposed to a crappy one.

DESCRIBE THE FEELING OF BEING ONSTAGE.

It feels like being in a bubble bath for slightly too long.

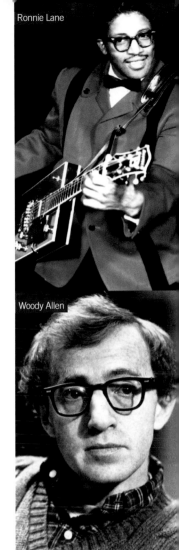

Ronnie Lane

Woody Allen

Donald Sutherland

KEREN ANN

Keren Ann is a peripatetic creature—she has both Dutch and Israeli citizenship, lives in Paris and New York, and spends most of her time traveling the world, playing her delicate, captivating songs. The cosmopolitan singer has released solo albums in both French and English (and is equally eloquent in both), and also has a side project with Icelandic musician Bardi Johansson called Lady & Bird (their self-titled first album, which featured ethereal covers of the Velvet Underground's "Stephanie Says" and M.A.S.H. theme tune "Suicide is Painless," was released in 2006). Her American breakthrough was 2003's *Not Going Anywhere*—but clearly, this girl is going places.

Billie Holiday

WHO OR WHAT FIRST MADE YOU WANT TO MAKE MUSIC?

It must have been a blend of sounds that were playing at home. I was obsessed with Serge Gainsbourg and John Lennon.

WHAT ALBUMS OR SONGS HAVE BEEN MOST INFLUENTIAL FOR YOU?

"The Times They Are A-Changin'" and "Boots of Spanish Leather" by Bob Dylan; _Let's Get Lost_ by Chet Baker; _Histoire de Melody Nelson_ by Serge Gainsbourg; _The White Album_ by the Beatles; and _Thriller_ by Michael Jackson.

WHAT WAS THE FIRST RECORD YOU EVER OWNED?

Tapestry by Carole King.

WHAT WAS YOUR FIRST CONCERT?

Ray Charles at the Caesarea Amphitheatre. My older sister took me.

WHAT INSTRUMENTS DO YOU PLAY AND HOW DID YOU LEARN?

Guitar, clarinet, keyboards. I also play some other instruments, but badly. I learned with a book, but I did take a few guitar lessons when I was a teenager.

WHAT ARTIST WHOM YOU NEVER GOT TO SEE PERFORM WOULD YOU LOVE TO HAVE SEEN?

Chet Baker and Billie Holiday.

IF YOU COULD COLLABORATE WITH ANYONE, WHO WOULD IT BE?

Bob Marley.

FIRST RECORD YOU REACH FOR WHEN YOU NEED TO BE CHEERED UP?

The Mamas and The Papas Greatest Hits.

FIRST RECORD YOU REACH FOR WHEN YOU WOULD RATHER NOT BE CHEERED UP?

The Ghost Of Tom Joad by Bruce Springsteen.

WHAT ARE YOUR BIGGEST NONMUSICAL INFLUENCES?

Romain Gary, Alfred Hitchcock, John Ford, and the desert.

WHAT'S YOUR FAVORITE MUSIC MOVIE?

This Is Spinal Tap!

WHAT ADVICE DO YOU HAVE FOR PEOPLE WHO WANT TO START BANDS?

Always choose honest over cool.

DESCRIBE THE FEELING OF BEING ONSTAGE.

It's like tightrope-walking over a pool. No one will get hurt if you fall, but you still can't allow it.

John Lennon

Alfred Hitchcock

Bob Marley

Jane Birkin and Serge Gainsbourg

THIS IS
Spinal Tap

SARA QUIN

TEGAN & SARA

smashing pumpkins · siamese dream

BORN IN THE U.S.A. BRUCE SPRINGSTEEN

It is easy to imagine Tegan and Sara as energetic eight-year-olds running circles around each other in the backyard and inventing complicated, imaginative games. The Canadian twins have been making music together since the tender age of fifteen, and their impetuous spirit is still going strong. Tegan & Sara's songs bristle with raw emotion and enthusiasm, and with five albums already under their belts, the duo remains as inspired and inde-fatigable as ever.

WHAT SPARKED YOUR DESIRE TO MAKE MUSIC?

I always really loved music but it was probably when I was about fourteen and started seeing local punk rock bands at the community center. As much as I loved music like Bruce Springsteen, Led Zeppelin, and the Police growing up, I never thought to myself: "I wanna be the Police." But when I started going to see the punk rock shows, I remember thinking: I could do this.

WHAT WAS THE FIRST INSTRUMENT YOU PICKED UP?

Both Tegan and I have played piano since we were little kids. I loved it, especially in high school when I had a teacher I really liked. I had been in piano lessons since elementary school and piano teachers were kind of like nurses. But this lady's students were so cool. At the piano recital, I remember the older kids playing the compositions they had written themselves instead of classical pieces that they had just practiced over and over. But when Tegan and I were about fifteen, we started playing guitar. That was different because it was about improvising, doing whatever we could to make decent sound. We taught ourselves.

WHAT WAS THE FIRST RECORD THAT YOU EVER BOUGHT?

Smashing Pumpkins' *Siamese Dream*. I was in seventh grade.

HOW DID THE STUFF YOU WERE LISTENING TO AS A TEENAGER FILTER DOWN INTO YOUR OWN MUSIC?

Well, when we first started playing guitar in about '94, we were listening to everything that was coming out of Seattle when it broke into the mainstream, like Nirvana, the Meat Puppets, Smashing Pumpkins...but we also listened to all the Riot Grrrl stuff. I find when I'm talking to younger kids now, everything is all about the Internet and I'm like, how the hell did we, suburban kids living in Calgary, Alberta, discover Bikini Kill and freakin' L7? But you just did, you found it through compilations. Or someone at a record store would be like, "You look like these people, you should listen to the music they make." So because of the stuff we were listening to, our first Tegan-&-Sara–esque project was a punk band we called Plunk, because we were like punk, but lighter. We would just play really loud. Later we started focusing more on songwriting.

WHAT WAS THE FIRST CONCERT THAT HAD A BIG EFFECT ON YOU?

Bruce Springsteen. My parents were really over-the-moon Springsteen fans. I'd go to peoples' houses and their parents would have a "Home Is Where the Heart Is" embroidery on the wall; we had this gigantic photo of the *Born in the U.S.A.* cover in the front entryway in our house. So that was our first concert, and it was amazing. I remember the lights going down and everyone going "BRUCE!" I thought they were booing and I was like, "Why are they booing already? Wow." But I totally loved it.

WHAT ALBUMS HAVE BEEN MOST SIGNIFICANT TO YOU?

Bruce Springsteen's first album, *Greetings From Asbury Park, N.J.* I don't know why. I don't think Springsteen fans usually pick that record. It was definitely the wordiest of his records. I remember when I first started writing songs I would write, like, ten pages of lyrics for one song because I thought that's what I should do. Also, Smashing Pumpkins, *Siamese Dream*. It was literally the first record I bought and I was totally obsessed. That was the band I slept in the parking lot to get concert tickets for and had posters of on my ceiling. That was that band that did it for me when I was a kid, and I'll never get over that.

DO YOU HAVE A FAVORITE MUSIC MOVIE, VIDEO, OR DOCUMENTARY?

A movie called *Phantom of the Paradise*. It was kind of a spoof on *Phantom of the Opera*, as a '70s rock opera. Brian de Palma directed it, and Paul Williams plays this character Swan who is this, like, disfigured musician... he actually wrote all the music in it. The movie was a little bit above us when we first saw it, but the record we loved. When we got older we went back to it, and we were like, "Everybody in this movie and making this movie was on drugs," but we were dancing to it when we were five, completely oblivious.

WHO ARE YOUR STYLE ICONS?

I find that as I'm getting older, I look at people who, back in the day, I would never have thought were cool. I was looking at an old record cover for Elton John recently, and I'm like, Elton John was rad, like, *amazing*. We're so used to hearing how David Bowie was cool and The Clash were cool, but Elton John was really, really cool!

Sting and the Police

Bruce Springsteen

Elton John

LUIZA SÁ

CSS

CSS, or Cansei de Ser Sexy (which translates from Portuguese as "tired of being sexy," a phrase they pinched from something Beyoncé once said in an interview), is made up of five girls (Lovefoxxx, Luiza Sá, Ana Rezende, Iracema Trevisan, and Carolina Parra), and one guy (Adriano Cintra) from São Paulo, Brazil, who play arty, sexed-up, multilingual, electro-dance-punk. We think their humorous pop culture-inspired songs, no-holds-barred performances, irrepressible enthusiasm, and creative iconoclasm make them the most fun thing to come out of South America since bossa nova. Multi-instrumentalist Luiza Sá plays drums, guitar, and keyboards—and, when the band started out, was still in college, studying art.

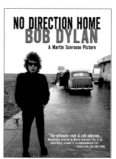

WHAT WAS THE SPARK THAT MADE YOU WANT TO MAKE MUSIC?

Music has always been a really big part of my life. My parents had a really big record collection—my whole family is really into music, so we always had it playing at home. I was a complete Beatlemaniac when I was a little kid. I think some people are just born with an affinity for music.

WHAT INSTRUMENT DID YOU FIRST PLAY?

My dad gave me a really cool old Casiotone keyboard when I was ten, and then when I was thirteen, I asked him for a guitar. It's the one I still play today!

DID YOU TEACH YOURSELF?

Yeah. I just worked songs out myself—I never took a lesson. I actually think it's freeing to not know how to read music or not know the theory or the rules; it makes you more creative. It doesn't matter how you do it: You're an artist, making art.

WHAT WAS THE FIRST CONCERT YOU EVER WENT TO?

The first concert that really changed my life was Madonna. She was doing an open-air show in a stadium for like eighty thousand people, and I told my mom that I wanted to go so badly, and she took me. It was amazing. I was only ten, and it really made quite an impression on me. It was like a Broadway production…but also this incredible pop concert.

WHAT THREE RECORDS HAVE BEEN MOST SIGNIFICANT TO YOU OVER THE YEARS?

The Velvet Underground and Nico. It was the first punk album, even though it's not really punk, it's pop. I think it's an album that really defines everything that came after it. It's just the greatest thing ever: Lou Reed and Nico and Andy Warhol in New York in the '60s, all coming together, like, that is so amazing and cool. The songs are really simple, and I think that's incredibly hard to do. That's the same reason that I really appreciate Cat Power now—her songs are so simple, but so powerful.

PJ Harvey, *Rid of Me.* There are a lot of albums that I really admire that I never feel like listening to, but I listen to PJ Harvey almost every day.

The Strokes, *Is This It?* I think that was a very special album, and it meant a lot to my generation when it came out.

It's really unpretentious and tiny—it's only forty minutes—but it's got such a perfect sound. It's a modern album, but it's already a classic, and that can't be said of many albums.

IF YOU COULD COLLABORATE WITH ANYONE, WHO WOULD IT BE?

We have been so lucky to have already collaborated with many people who have been important to me. We've played with Donita Sparks from L7, who is someone who really inspired me when I was younger, as did Hole and all of those girls. So that was just wonderful to be on the same stage with her. Jarvis Cocker sang with us once, too, and so did Beth [Ditto] from The Gossip, and Peaches…. These are all people who I really admire and who made me want to make music, so it's just crazy to me. But I guess if you're involved in something you believe in, you're going to end up attracting and meeting people who might once have seemed so far away or out of reach.

DO YOU HAVE A FAVORITE MUSIC DOCUMENTARY OR MOVIE?

I love that collection of Sonic Youth videos [*Corporate Ghost: Videos 1990–2002*], and I recently saw Martin Scorsese's documentary about Bob Dylan, *No Direction Home*, which traces his whole life and all of the people who influenced him and how his music impacted the world. It's really good.

WHO HAS HAD THE BIGGEST INFLUENCE ON YOUR STYLE?

Growing up, I'd say it was the characters in John Waters's movies. They were so cool. And Chloë Sevigny in the movie *Gummo* was a pretty big deal to me—I just thought she had the most amazing style.

WHAT ADVICE WOULD YOU GIVE TO SOMEONE WHO WANTS TO START A BAND NOW?

First of all, have fun. Do whatever you think is good, and don't give a damn about what other people say. Be a nice person and realize that people will give you creative advice, but do what you believe in. And don't be afraid of things going wrong—have low expectations. Don't rush it. Don't think that as soon as you write a song you need to play a show or have a record deal; don't expect to get successful overnight. It's work, you know? And just because you don't get famous right away, that doesn't mean that you're not any good or that it's never going to happen. Have faith.

Chloë Sevigny in *Gummo*

Madonna

Traci Lords in *CRY-BABY*

KATE JACKSON

The Long Blondes sprang onto the U.K. music scene in 2006 with *Someone To Drive You Home*, a set of smart, stylish songs that name-drop such band heroines as Edie Sedgwick and Anna Karina. And with her fondness for vintage neck scarves, pencil skirts, and high heels, frontwoman Kate Jackson has herself become something of a fashion icon for girls who love dressed-up glamour just as much as they love getting down 'n' dirty on the dance floor.

WHO OR WHAT FIRST SPARKED YOUR DESIRE TO BE IN A BAND?

It was watching the Freddie Mercury tribute concert in 1992. I really got obsessed with Guns N' Roses after that. My mum and I even went to L.A. so I could take photos of all the clubs on Sunset where Guns N' Roses used to play! I actually wanted to be a guitarist but I was never very good—my nails are too long to play guitar.

WHAT WAS THE FIRST RECORD YOU EVER OWNED?

The first 7-inch I bought was "Manic Monday" by the Bangles in 1985. The first album was probably a Kylie album.

WHAT DID YOU LISTEN TO AS A TEEN-AGER AND HOW DID IT AFFECT YOUR MUSIC LATER?

I was a teenager during the Britpop years in the U.K. and it was great. I used to be known as "Kate the punk" 'round town 'cos I wore these holey pink tights, big boots, and a leather miniskirt. That all changed when I discovered Suede. Suede and Pulp became my obsession as a teenager and those bands have certainly influenced the Long Blondes both lyrically and stylistically.

WHAT ALBUMS HAVE BEEN MOST SIGNIFICANT TO YOU?

Suede, *Suede*. It changed my life. It made me think that I could escape my small town and have a life in the big city.

Pulp, *Intro [The Gift Recordings]*. I wouldn't have moved to Sheffield without this record.

Lee Hazlewood, *Cowboy in Sweden*. This is my favorite album. I love how tongue-in-cheek Lee Hazlewood is, and the dynamic he has with the Swedish singer Nina Lizell on this record. It was a [Swedish] TV series too but I've never seen it.

The Fall, *This Nation's Saving Grace*. When I was a teenager, I felt like only me and my friends knew about the Fall. It was like being a member of a private club, talking about Fall records all the time. There are so many great Fall albums, but this works best as a whole.

Le Tigre, *Le Tigre*: This was the only good record released in 1999 and it got me through my first year of university. A difficult time for me, but a terrible time for British music. All the good bands were American. I met Dorian and Emma when I played "Hot Topic" at the Sheffield Barfly when I used to D.J. there. They came up and talked to me because they were amazed someone else liked Le Tigre!

WHAT ARTIST WHOM YOU NEVER GOT TO SEE PERFORM WOULD YOU MOST LOVE TO SEE?

I had the chance to see Nina Simone at Nick Cave's Meltdown in 1999 and I couldn't go. She died shortly afterwards. I wish I had seen Madonna on the Blonde Ambition tour, and I wish wish wish I had seen Guns N' Roses but I was too young to go.

WHAT RECORD ALWAYS MAKES YOU WANT TO DANCE?

Shocking Blue, "Send Me a Postcard." Another D.J.ing favorite.

WHAT RECORD DO YOU REACH FOR WHEN YOU'RE FEELING MELANCHOLY?

Neil Young, *On the Beach*. It makes everything drift away.

WHO IS THE MOST OVERLOOKED OR UNDERAPPRECIATED ARTIST, IN YOUR OPINION?

There was a singer called Evie Sands who sounded like Dusty Springfield. She should have been a huge star.

IF YOU COULD COLLABORATE WITH ANYONE (LIVING OR DEAD), WHO WOULD IT BE?

It would have to be Lee Hazlewood. I would love to sit on his knee and sing a duet with him. But I think he only likes blondes.

WHO ARE YOUR STYLE ICONS?

Diana Dors, Faye Dunaway as Bonnie Parker, Sherilyn Fenn as Audrey Horne in *Twin Peaks*, Jarvis Cocker.

DO YOU HAVE A FAVORITE MUSIC FILM, DOCUMENTARY, OR VIDEO?

I think all the ABBA videos are great. Music videos now just look so polished. ABBA did everything they needed in a white room with a couple of chairs and a lighting rig.

DESCRIBE THE FEELING OF BEING ONSTAGE.

If the crowd is really into it, then your adrenaline just takes over and you find yourself lost in the moment; but if one or two things go wrong then you start noticing everything and thinking too much. It's the best and worst place in the world.

WHAT ADVICE DO YOU HAVE FOR PEOPLE STARTING BANDS?

Don't listen to anyone who says you have to follow a certain formula or process to become successful, like finding a manager before you get signed or playing at a certain venue ten times. Every band has a different path.

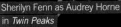

Sherilyn Fenn as Audrey Horne in *Twin Peaks*

ABBA

Faye Dunaway as Bonnie Parker In *Bonnie and Clyde*

BAT FOR LASHES
NATASHA KHAN

Since the release of her 2007 debut album, *Fur and Gold*, British singer-songwriter Natasha Khan, a.k.a. Bat For Lashes, has been compared to the likes of Kate Bush, Björk, and Cat Power. But with her ethereal, folk-music-and-poetry-inflected songs, which conjure a magical world populated by horses, wizards, court jesters, and fairies (she was a nursery-school teacher before she started her band), she's definitely following her own, very idiosyncratic path. And her headbands rock.

WHO OR WHAT FIRST MADE YOU WANT TO MAKE MUSIC?

James Taylor, who made me realize that music could be an emotionally driven art, and watching movies like *The Wizard of Oz* when I was growing up. I started writing cheesy love songs when I was listening to a lot of George Michael…. I really loved Courtney Love and was influenced a lot by her at first, but then I realized I wasn't very good at screaming, so I started listening to music that was more feminine, like Joni Mitchell.

WHAT THREE ALBUMS HAVE BEEN MOST INFLUENTIAL TO YOU?

Probably *Fleetwood Mac*, Michael Jackson's *Thriller*, and *The Very Best of Prince*. But I also like Bananarama!

WHAT WAS THE FIRST CONCERT YOU EVER WENT TO?

Michael Jackson at Wembley Stadium, when I was seven years old. I thought it was wicked, even though the stage was so far away and he was so tiny that it could've been anyone up there. What overwhelmed me was the sound of the crowd. It was the first time I'd ever heard such a response to music.

HOW WOULD YOU DESCRIBE THE FEELING YOU GET NOW WHEN YOU GO ONSTAGE?

I've learned that the more crazy and hyped the crowd gets, the harder it is to remember what you're doing. It's really important to guide your audience through a performance, to bring them down and then take them up, and take your time. Otherwise, you kind of get washed away by all of the adrenaline. It's difficult not to let that take over.

WHAT INSTRUMENTS DO YOU PLAY AND HOW DID YOU LEARN THEM?

I play the piano, the autoharp, guitar, and drums. I'm most comfortable with the piano; it's like an extension of my bones. I started when I was about seven, but it took a few years before I understood that I could create my own music with it.

WHO ARE YOUR STYLE ICONS?

Patricia Arquette is the sexiest woman that ever lived! I really liked her style in *True Romance*—she was L.A. trashy but with a little bit of a film noir edge. Also Nico and Jane Birkin. I like those sort of '60s bohemian women. And Cleopatra…. I like to think I have a defined sense of style. I make all my own headdresses and I'm in charge of all the visual aspects of what I do—it's in my contract. I do all the illustrations, Web site design, and album art. It's really important to me.

FIRST RECORD YOU REACH FOR WHEN YOU NEED TO BE CHEERED UP?

Probably something by Bobby Brown, Stevie Nicks, or cheesy Heart songs. If I'm feeling a bit out of sorts, I just put on something I can really move to.

FIRST RECORD YOU REACH FOR WHEN YOU WOULD RATHER NOT BE CHEERED UP?

The Cure, *Disintegration,* or maybe a Nico album.

BEST NONMUSICAL INFLUENCES?

Film is probably my biggest influence. *Donnie Darko, Buffalo '66,* and *The Virgin Suicides* all came out when I was in my early twenties, and had such a brilliant influence on me. Writing songs is a very visual process for me, so films and the music in them can be so powerful. Eventually, I'd love to score a film.

WHAT'S YOUR ADVICE FOR PEOPLE WANTING TO START BANDS?

Know yourself before you embark on it because it really tests the fabric of who you are. If you want your music to be honest, then you need to really know what you want to say. I think it's also important to be free and nonjudgmental, and not be embarrassed about who you are. It's easy to follow the crowd and do what the mainstream is doing. Having your own path is key.

Elizabeth Taylor as Cleopatra

Patricia Arquette in *True Romance*

Judy Garland in *The Wizard of OZ*

Merrill Beth Nisker is a marvel of self-transformation. Before she adopted the persona of Peaches, she was an elementary school music teacher in her native Toronto (where she was Leslie Feist's roommate). She did her first tour by herself, sleeping in her car, with nothing but an electronic beatbox to back her up onstage. But what she lacked in professional amenities she more than made up for with, her, er, unique musical style. This Peach is lewd, crotch-grabbingly crude, and brazenly in-your-face: Her genre-skewing electro-hip-hop-rock songs revolve around sex, gender identity, and politics, with titles like "Lovertits" and "Shake Yer Dix"—you get the picture. Since those heady early days, she's gone on to collaborate with the likes of Iggy Pop and Yoko Ono, open for mammoth acts like Björk and Marilyn Manson, and record three thoroughly filthy, absolutely fantastic albums.

Grace Jones

WHO OR WHAT FIRST MADE YOU WANT TO MAKE MUSIC?

No one or nothing in particular. I just couldn't stop singing and dancing as a young child.

NAME THE FIVE RECORDS THAT HAVE BEEN THE MOST INFLUENTIAL FOR YOU.

The Stooges, *The Stooges*; Lauryn Hill, *The Miseducation of Lauryn Hill*; PJ Harvey, *To Bring You My Love*; Kraftwerk, *Trans-Europe Express*; and Salt-n-Pepa, *Hot, Cool & Vicious*.

WHAT WAS THE FIRST RECORD YOU OWNED?

Bad Girls, by Donna Summer.

FIRST CONCERT YOU WENT TO?

Gladys Knight and the Pips, when I was six years old.

WHAT INSTRUMENTS DO YOU PLAY AND HOW DID YOU LEARN?

Guitars, electronics, and keyboards. I taught myself. I just played until it sounded like something I would want to hear.

WHO ARE YOUR STYLE ICONS?

Grace Jones, The Runaways, and Poison Ivy.

DO YOU HAVE A FAVORITE OUTFIT YOU'VE WORN ONSTAGE?

Yeah. White leather shorts with a jacket to match.

WHAT ARTIST WHOM YOU NEVER GOT TO SEE PERFORM WOULD YOU LOVE TO HAVE SEEN?

Prince, around the time of *Purple Rain*.

IF YOU COULD COLLABORATE WITH ANYONE, WHO WOULD IT BE?

I would borrow Daft Punk's lighting show.

WHAT RECORD ALWAYS MAKES YOU WANT TO DANCE?

ESG, *Come Away with ESG*

WHAT RECORD ALWAYS MAKES YOU SAD?

One of my favorites: *To Bring You My Love*, PJ Harvey.

WHO IS THE MOST OVERLOOKED ARTIST, IN YOUR OPINION?

Girlschool needs to be recognized! They were a South London all-girl metal-rock band in the late '70s, early '80s.

BEST CONCERT YOU'VE EVER BEEN TO?

Guitar Wolf in Toronto in 1998.

BIGGEST NONMUSICAL INFLUENCE ON YOUR SONGWRITING?

Bike riding!

WHAT'S YOUR FAVORITE MUSIC MOVIE?

Scorsese's *The King of Comedy*.

WHAT ADVICE DO YOU HAVE FOR PEOPLE WHO WANT TO GET INTO MUSIC?

Don't be afraid. Get drunk, get together with friends, and bang on things.

Prince

Girlschool

JUSTINE D

Justine D is the chic mastermind
behind New York's monthly party
event Motherfucker, which has got-
ten bigger and wilder since it
kicked off in 2000. She started
off as a promoter and D.J., and
now juggles many titles on her
extensive résumé, including being
the events director for Brooklyn
venue Studio B. She released her
first DJ mix compilation CD, *RVNG
PRSNTS MX5: Justine D*, in 2007,
revealing her love for some fan-
tastically arcane artists (Gob-
lin, Malaria!, Death in June) as
well as some of the all-time great
dance floor-fillers (the Cars, Chic,
David Bowie).

BLUE TRAIN

john coltrane
blue note 53428

bauhaus

HOW DID YOU GET YOUR START?

Purely by accident. I was asked to start promoting by a good friend of mine at the time. He was a promoter for a new indie night at a large club and I was supplying him with half of his guest list...[so he] asked me to be a part of it. Within four months, I was director of the night and running every aspect. I was twenty-two.

WHAT'S YOUR FAVORITE BAND YOU'VE EVER SEEN PLAY?

It has always been Kraftwerk. The stage show and the music inspire me artistically and create such an exciting atmosphere in the room. In my teenage years, I was also a fanatical fan of Morrissey and the Cure. They'll always remind me of high school heartbreak... oh, so dramatic!

WHAT'S YOUR PRIMARY SOURCE FOR FINDING NEW MUSIC?

YouTube, MySpace, recommendations from friends, and eBay. You can actually learn a lot from eBay. I buy a lot of my records on there; if you take a look at a record seller's other auctions, you can usually find out about some new music. And when I say new, I don't mean new bands, but songs from bands you know, which you've never heard before.

HOW DID YOU LEARN TO D.J.?

My D.J. career started several months after my promotions career. I had been a record collector for several years and a girlfriend of mine with a weekly party asked me to spin for her. This was a totally new concept for me...getting paid $40 to play records I adore out in public? It seemed like an exciting idea. She taught me the basics of using a mixer and two turntables thirty minutes before my two-hour set. It was a little unnerving, but I was pretty hooked after my first experience.

AS SOMEONE WHO IS OUT BEING SEEN EVERY NIGHT, YOU'VE DEVELOPED A DISTINCTIVE STYLE. WHO ARE YOUR FASHION ICONS?

David Bowie, The Baader Meinhof Group, models in Helmut Newton photos (1977 through '83). A lot of my inspiration stems from older fashion labels, like Halston, Biba, Vivienne Westwood. I also quite like Bernard Sumner's fashion sensibility while he was in Joy Division, Diane Keaton in *Manhattan*, Ali MacGraw in *Love Story*, and Catherine Deneuve in *Belle De Jour*.

WHAT ADVICE WOULD YOU GIVE TO PEOPLE WHO WANT TO GET INTO PARTY PROMOTING AND D.J.ING?

For D.J.ing, BUY RECORDS. Do the research, support the bands you love, and buy their music. Do not be an MP3 D.J.; there is little skill involved, because the programs do most of the work for you. While technology is a must to survive in the modern age, it's important to preserve the original methods of D.J.ing and music collecting. If you must, buy CDs, but I always recommend vinyl. My best advice for promoting is to be honest, do not stiff people on money, and do it for the love of music and for the good of the scene you're a part of—not for local fame, which is fleeting anyway.

WHAT RECORDS HAVE BEEN MOST INFLUENTIAL TO YOU?

John Coltrane, *Blue Train*
This album makes me feel sad about life and yet grateful to be alive. It's quite possibly one of the most romantic albums ever and I've been able to do a lot of soul searching while listening to it. Incredibly smooth and perfect for listening to in the dark, preferably when I'm alone.

Bauhaus, *The Sky's Gone Out*
This album was one of the first I bought with my own money. I listened to it when my ears were young and unaffected. I had never heard such a dramatic and experimental album before. The chanting, looping, and strings were pretty life-altering.

David Bowie, *Hunky Dory*
The first David Bowie album I ever listened to from beginning to end. Epic, rather quirky and folky. Bowie before Ziggy Stardust but both eras are great.

Helmut Newton model

Diane Keaton in *Manhattan*

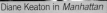

Model in Biba in front of Biba Boutique

David Bowie

MISSHAPES
LEIGH LEZARK

Hipster D.J. threesome the MisShapes—Leigh Lezark, Greg Krelenstein, and Geordon Nicol—began throwing their notoriously stylish and star-studded Saturday night soirees in 2004. The parties quickly became a staple of New York nightlife for the young and the restless, generating endless buzz and attracting a huge fan following that established the trio as some of the country's most in-demand event hosts. Lezark, who is the most photographed MisShape, was raised in Toms River, New Jersey, and started hitting the New York party scene when she was only seventeen.

HOW DID YOU FIRST GET INTO PARTY PROMOTING AND D.J.ING?

I had tons of records growing up. I had a serious obsession with really new bands, underground music, and older popular artists. I moved to New York when I was seventeen and loved going to dance parties. The two just kind of fell into place: Friends of mine were D.J.s and taught me how to use the equipment, and soon after that I was D.J.ing on my own all the time.

WHAT MUSIC WERE YOU MOST INSPIRED BY WHEN YOU WERE GROWING UP? WHOSE POSTERS DID YOU HAVE UP ON YOUR WALLS?

The artists I was really inspired by didn't have wall posters. I was most inspired by Bikini Kill, then later Le Tigre, Huggy Bear, Siouxsie and the Banshees, Refused, PJ Harvey, the (International) Noise Conspiracy, Hole, Nirvana…the list goes on and on.

WHAT'S YOUR PRIMARY SOURCE FOR NEW MUSIC?

The Internet. In a few clicks you can research a new band, preview their songs, hunt down the tracks you like, burn a few CDs and you're good for the night. That's not all it takes to be a D.J.—you have to have a lot of knowledge of music—but the Internet makes obscure bands more accessible.

WHAT RECORD DO YOU KNOW WILL ALWAYS MAKE PEOPLE GO CRAZY ON THE DANCE FLOOR?

It varies. People get bored of songs, so every few months there will be a song that everyone really gels into, whether it be a mainstream song or underground. My job is to find the next earworm song before it falls into the "Hey Ya" wayside.

HAVE YOU EVER PLAYED SOMETHING AND HAD IT COMPLETELY BOMB?

Oh yes. I'm sure every D.J. has moments where a song just doesn't fit in, followed by a few seconds of sheer panic. However, you get over it, change songs and continue.

WHAT ARE THE MOST REQUESTED SONGS?

Usually older '80s songs that people know every word of.

WHAT'S THE MOST REQUESTED SONG THAT YOU REFUSE TO SPIN?

Anything Michael Jackson, people go nuts for him.

WHAT CELEB OR MUSICIAN WHO HAS COME TO MISSHAPES HAS MADE YOU THE MOST STARSTRUCK?

I was fascinated to meet people like Madonna and Yoko Ono; they were really down to earth and jumped behind the D.J. booth and did their thing. Kathleen Hanna and Jarvis Cocker are musical icons of mine. I was very excited to meet them on well.

WHAT ADVICE WOULD YOU GIVE TO PEOPLE STARTING PARTIES?

DON'T. Just kidding, my advice would be to be nice to everyone, don't make enemies. Take risks with music you play. And be careful talking to the press.

WHAT WOULD YOU SAY IS THE SECRET TO MISSHAPES' SUCCESS?

That's easy. Our friends have been the secret to MisShapes' success. They've shown so much love and support since day one.

Jarvis Cocker

Siouxsie Sioux

Yoko Ono with John Lennon

THE RAVEONETTES
SHARIN FOO

As one half of the Danish duo the Raveonettes (their name was inspired by the Buddy Holly song "Rave On"), which she formed in 2001 with guitarist Sune Rose Wagner, Sharin Foo is, hands down, one of the classiest young ladies ever to play bleak, brooding rock 'n' roll. The band's sound—something like what vintage girl groups, Elvis, and surf punk would sound like if filtered through the droning feedback haze of the Velvet Underground and the Jesus and Mary Chain—is as unique and striking as Foo herself. Singing close harmonies with Wagner, she infuses even their darkest lyrics with a sultry elegance, just as her Nico-esque blonde hair and (usually black) retro dresses add lashings of classic film star glamour to the Raveonettes' live shows.

WHAT WAS THE INITIAL SPARK THAT MADE YOU WANT TO GET INTO MUSIC?

I was drawn to the emotions that music inspires, and since playing and singing came fairly naturally to me, I just sort of found myself here.

HOW OLD WERE YOU WHEN YOU FIRST PICKED UP ANY INSTRUMENT, AND DID YOU TEACH YOURSELF TO PLAY?

I was brought up in a very musical home, so there was always a piano and a guitar around, and someone to show me something new.

WHAT MUSIC DID YOU LISTEN TO AS A TEENAGER AND HOW HAS IT AFFECTED THE MUSIC YOU MAKE NOW?

Fleetwood Mac, David Bowie, Pink Floyd, the Beatles, Joni Mitchell, The Cure. Obviously, my musical tastes have evolved over time and once being a musician becomes your profession, being more critical and discerning of what you spend your time listening to is almost part of the job description. But the excitement of hearing or playing something really good and genuine never changes. You tend to naturally discard what no longer has relevance to you.

WHAT WAS THE FIRST ALBUM YOU EVER OWNED?

Neil Young, *Harvest*.

WHAT WAS THE FIRST CONCERT YOU EVER WENT TO?

Prince.

WHAT ARE YOUR ALL-TIME FAVOR-ITE RECORDS AND WHY?

Bob Dylan, *Bringing It All Back Home*. It is still such a modern, complex, raw fusion of elements illuminated by words you can live off for a lifetime.

The Velvet Underground and Nico. This remains the ultimate ratio of pop to menace.

Scott Walker, *Scott 3*. He really exists outside of all categorization and no one tells a story in a more bizarre and yet accessible way.

DO YOU HAVE A FAVORITE MUSIC BOOK, VIDEO, OR DOCUMENTARY?

Rock And the Pop Narcotic by Joe Carducci, Godard's 1968 *Sympathy For The Devil*, and the Dylan documentary *Don't Look Back* by D.A. Pennebaker.

YOU'VE ALREADY WORKED WITH SOME AMAZING PEOPLE, LIKE RONNIE SPECTOR, MOE TUCKER AND MARTIN REV, BUT WHO ELSE—LIVING OR DEAD—WOULD YOU WANT TO COLLABORATE WITH?

Scott Walker; Michelangelo Antonioni; [Danish painter] Tal R.

WHAT SONG ALWAYS CHEERS YOU UP/MAKES YOU WANT TO DANCE?

The Smiths, "There Is A Light That Never Goes Out."

WHAT RECORD DO YOU REACH FOR WHEN YOU'RE IN A SAD OR REFLEC-TIVE MOOD?

One of two Talk Talk records: *Laughing Stock* or *Spirit of Eden*.

WHO ARE YOUR STYLE ICONS?

Monica Vitti, Lee Miller, [modernist furniture designer] Eileen Gray, and Marlene Dietrich.

WHAT ADVICE DO YOU HAVE FOR PEOPLE ARE STARTING BANDS NOW?

Love the music you love, play the music you play, and never let outside agendas change what those things are. You have an exponentially greater chance of success if you follow these principles than if you indulge in any second-guessing.

Monica Vitti

Marlene Dietrich

Joni Mitchell

THEY MAY BE MORE LIKELY TO BE
IPOD PLAYLISTS OR CDS THAN
ACTUAL CASSETTE TAPES THESE
DAYS, BUT MIXTAPES REMAIN
DEFINING STATEMENTS OF MUSICAL
INTENT, WHETHER THEY'RE DESIGNED
TO WOO A MEMBER OF THE OPPO-
SITE SEX, AS THE SOUND TRACK
FOR A PARTY, OR SIMPLY AS PER-
SONAL TIME CAPSULES OF BEST-
LOVED SONGS. MIXTAPES ARE A
STAPLE OF *NYLON*, SO OF COURSE,
FOR *PLAY* WE ASKED SOME OF OUR
FAVORITE MUSICIANS TO COMPILE
THEIR ALL-TIME FAVORITE SONGS.

CHAPTER **3**

KATE NASH

There's a bit of a fairy-tale element to Kate Nash's backstory. After being rejected from drama school, she fell down a flight of stairs and broke her foot, which prompted her to turn to songwriting (on guitar, piano, and synthesizer) while she recuperated. After playing a few self-booked gigs in pubs and loading some of her songs onto MySpace, she was heralded by none other than Lily Allen as being the "next big thing." And poof—she was. Buoyed by her characteristic storytelling, realistically gritty lyrics, and informal, heavily-London-accented singing style, Nash's single "Foundations" crashed onto the U.K. charts at Number 2 in the summer of 2007 (just before her twentieth birthday); her Number 1 debut album, Made of Bricks, followed a few months later. She cites some of her influences as "bored teenagers, PJ Harvey, Sex Pistols, Roald Dahl, and having the blues." Here are a few more, of the downloadable variety.

1 MOLDY PEACHES

"Nothing Came Out" —
Moldy Peaches
I love this album. It's really lo-fi, funny, and cute. There is this one bit where you can hear that when Kimya Dawson is singing, she's cracking up.

2 BIKINI KILL

"Star-bellied Boy" — *Pussy Whipped*
My friend and I played this song yesterday. We were dancing around, and we cleared all the stuff off the bed and jumped on it until it was ruined. I'm obsessed with being a bit of a feminist at the moment. I love the whole Riot Grrrl punk movement, and Bikini Kill were really important.

3 BJÖRK

"Hyperballad" — *Post*
This was the first song that really got me into Björk—just imagining her in the mountains where it's really beautiful and really Björky—and she just throws stuff out the window and then imagines what she would feel like being thrown out. It's one of those songs you can just repeat and repeat, and get lost in.

4 BUZZCOCKS

"Ever Fallen in Love?" —
Singles Going Steady
I used to walk to my guitar lesson while playing this whole album. It was all I would listen to. That was when I first got into punk. I love this song's honesty—it's heartfelt and sweet. The thing I think some men get wrong is the idea that being a dick or being horrible makes you more masculine. Or that not showing how you feel is cool.

5 JONATHAN RICHMAN

"When She Kisses Me" —
Surrender to Jonathan
I just love his whole thing. He was obsessed with [the year] 1963 and he just wanted to write songs that sound like that. But his lyrics are so funny. I love stupid, cute stuff.

6 THE STROKES

"The End Has No End" —
Room on Fire
Everyone always says that *Room on Fire* isn't a good album. I hate that, because I think it's really good!

7 PEGGY SUE AND THE PIRATES

"Old Stupid Moon" — *(unrecorded)*
They are a band that I did my early gigs with, and they're going to come on tour with me. They're two fumbly little girls with the voices of old ladies. Brilliant!

8 MINUTEMEN

"Do You Want New Wave or Do You Want The Truth?" —
Double Nickels on the Dime
Another punk band not giving a fuck and not being afraid to say stuff, which I like.

EISLEY

Eisley could show the Partridge clan a thing or two. Consisting of four siblings and one cousin, the Texas-based quintet keep it all in the (talented) family. They released two full-length studio albums before any of the band members hit twenty, and have shared the stage with the likes of Hot Hot Heat, Coldplay, and Snow Patrol. Here sisters Chauntelle, Stacy, and Sherri DuPree deliver a Mix-Tape of the songs that inspire them most.

CHAUNTELLE DUPREE

1 IMOGEN HEAP
"Hide and Seek" — *Speak for Yourself*
I just love her voice in this song. There's no music but her vocals carry the melody. It's just brilliant!

2 M. WARD
"Let's Dance" — *Transfiguration of Vincent*
A David Bowie cover. It's romantic and sweet. I love it!

3 MODEST MOUSE
"The World at Large" — *Good News for People Who Love Bad News*
I love the flow of this song so much! It makes me happy no matter what.

STACY DUPREE

4 PAUL MCCARTNEY
"Junk" — *McCartney*
When I first heard this song I didn't recognize it as Paul McCartney because it had such a mysticism and melancholy to it. It's very beautiful and sentimental to me.

5 CAROLE KING
"So Far Away" — *Tapestry*
My parents always used to sing this and harmonize to each other. It brings back good memories.

6 FLEETWOOD MAC
"Silver Springs" — *Rumours*, Remastered Version
I love Stevie's voice on this song. So much hurt and jealousy in the way she sings the lyrics "Did you say that she's pretty?" and "Baby I don't wanna know." Absolutely amazing.

SHERRI DUPREE

7 NEUTRAL MILK HOTEL
"In the Aeroplane Over the Sea" — *In the Aeroplane Over the Sea*
This song will forever be my favorite song ever written. There is something so beautiful about it that it's almost painful.

8 THE BEATLES
"Oh! Darling" — *Abbey Road*
Paul McCartney sings this song with everything he's got and I love it to death. It's so gutsy and amazing.

9 NEW FOUND GLORY
"On My Mind" — *Coming Home*
It's about completely loving someone and cherishing the time you get to spend with them before you leave to go on tour again. Plus, my husband wrote it. Ha!

Z BERG

THE LIKE

Singer and guitarist Z Berg is one of three girls who comprise The Like. (Drummer Tennessee Thomas and bassist Charlotte Froom round out the trio.) These music prodigies started making music together before they were sixteen years old, and they instantly sounded more sophisticated than bands twice their age. Sweet, wistful, and dark—the Like are like no one else.

1 NILSSON

"Without You" — *Nilsson Schmilsson*
If ever you're in a long-dis-
tance relationship with someone, put this on a mixtape for
them. Just trust me.

2 ERIC BOGLE

"And The Band Played Waltzing
Matilda" — *Scraps of Paper*
Whatever you do, do not listen
to this song on a plane. You
will be inconsolable. The person
sitting next to you will think
you're insane. It is the most
absolutely heartbreaking song
ever written. Which, for me, is
probably the highest compliment
I can pay a song.

3 THE POGUES

"A Pair Of Brown Eyes" —
Rum, Sodomy & the Lash
Speaking of heartbreaking...oh
my lord. This is definitely not
plane music either.

4 JUDEE SILL

"The Kiss" *Heart Food*
You know that feeling when
you're so in love with someone
that it feels like your insides
are being pulled out of you by
an enormous magnet? That's what
Judee Sill's voice sounds like.

5 MARIANNE FAITHFULL

"Something Better" — *The Rolling
Stones Rock and Roll Circus*
One of those songs that makes
you feel like your life used to
be so much better, even if it
never was. And it's from *Rock
and Roll Circus*, so she's backed
by the best band EVER.

6 THE VERVE

"The Drugs Don't Work" —
Urban Hymns
I wish I had written this song
so badly that it's hard for me
to listen to it.

7 DORY PREVIN

"Lady with The Braid" —
Mythical Kings and Iguanas
It's so difficult to put into
words how incredible this song
is. It's like it covers the
entire range of human emotion
in four minutes. It really just
destroys me.

8 PRIMAL SCREAM

"Accelerator" — *Accelerator*
Find me a song that will blow out
your speakers quicker than this
baby and I'll take it off the
list. You can't do it, can you?

9 ROYAL TRUX

"Junkie Nurse" — *Royal Trux*
Neil Haggerty's voice sounds
like an animal dying in the best
way possible. This song is just
perfect, in the most spastic and
brutal way.

10 MARY HOPKIN

"Those Were the Days" — *Postcard*
Wistful gypsy music. I think
that about covers it.

THE WATSON TWINS

Chandra and Leigh Watson, a.k.a. the Watson Twins, sing exquisite, dulcet, country-inflected harmonies that can make your heart melt. The Louisville-born sisters first gained renown for singing backup with Jenny Lewis on her *Rabbit Fur Coat* solo album, but as they continue to prove, they're more than capable of holding the spotlight themselves.

1 BOB DYLAN

"She Belongs to Me" —
Bringing It All Back Home
"She's got everything she needs, she's an artist, she don't look back." Of course Dylan talks about his lady in a poetic display of affection.

2 SHIRLEY BROWN

"Woman to Woman" —
Woman to Woman
A quiet storm brought the Watson Twins and Shirley Brown together. Shirley = soul, and this song is undeniable! The spoken word breakdown takes this jam to another level.

3 WILLIE NELSON

"Whiskey River" —
Honeysuckle Rose [Sound track]
Our mom had lots of Willie records when we were growing up, and this song was part of the *Honeysuckle Rose* sound track. The whole album is ridiculously good.

4 SLINT

"Good Morning, Captain" —
Spiderland
Being from Louisville, this band represents like no other. *Spiderland* is a must-have for all modern-day indie rockers.

5 CROSBY, STILLS, NASH & YOUNG

"Almost Cut My Hair" — *Déjà Vu*
"I feel like letting my freak flag fly..." Instant anthem!

6 SIMON & GARFUNKEL

"America" — *Bookends*
A road trip song about new beginnings, love, and finding yourself. It's deep, man.

7 BANGLES

"Following" — *Different Light*
Although famous for songs like "Manic Monday" and "Walk Like An Egyptian," this tune takes the band to another dimension. Acoustic, honest, and a little bit on the dark side—just how we like 'em.

8 FREAKWATER

"My Old Drunk Friend" —
Feels Like the Third Time
These indie alt-country ladies from Louisville stir up memories of home, sticky summer nights, and a tall glass of bourbon.

9 ERYKAH BADU

"Green Eyes" — *Mama's Gun*
Girl got pipes! A little R&B, hip-hop, and Earth Mother all rolled into one.

10 THE MAMAS AND THE PAPAS

"Creeque Alley" — *Creeque Alley*
They had that California sound and amazing harmonies. We were taking notes.

AU REVOIR SIMONE

The ladies of Au Revoir Simone aren't French, and they aren't as delicate as their long–locked-loveliness might suggest. The Brooklyn-based trio was formed in a burst of inspiration on an idle afternoon, and Heather D'Angelo, Erika Forster, and Annie Hart decided to name their new band after a line in *Pee-wee's Big Adventure*. A perfect complement to Au Revoir Simone's whimsical, dreamy sound, their Mix-Tape includes a little bit of disco, a lot of love, and a song suitable for a hot air balloon.

1 YUME BITSU
"Song Nine" —
The Golden Vessyl of Sound
This song is hypnotic, entranc-
ing, and lovely. It may clock
in at an adventurous 8:09, but
listening to it is like falling
under a spell and forces me to
rewind and start afresh. The
gentle guitar lures you in with
a lolling, repetitive line on
top of a fading disharmonious
drum and squeal track; then
pure, quiet male vocals follow
to complete a picture with long
notes of a simple melody. A
picture of what? I don't know,
but I could bask in its glow
for days.

2 LIZ PHAIR
"Fuck and Run" — *Exile in Guyville*
Think about life, think about
love, and think about lyrics—and
know that what might look odd on
paper can cut straight to the
core of romance. "I want all
that stupid old shit like letters and sodas" is one of those
rare lines that encapsulates
just about everything I want
in a relationship, and Phair
juxtaposing that ideal with the
cold reality of her sex-fueled
existence is genius, concise,
and heart-wrenching. Love it.

3 MOUNTAIN GOATS
"California Song" — *Sweden*
"California Song" really stands
out among all the guitar-based
tracks on the record; the stark
simplicity of the single instrument—barely eking out all the
frequencies Darnielle squeezes
from it—echoes the loneli-
ness of the lyrics in a way
that an acoustic guitar rarely
can. I've held on to that ideal
for a long time.

4 JOHN LENNON
"Oh Yoko!" — *Imagine*
John Lennon is my hero, and this
song is pure joy. Perfect for
dancing around the living room
with someone you love. Also, easy
to sing along to as there aren't
very many lyrics to remember.

5 THE BEE GEES
"More Than A Woman" —
Saturday Night Fever [Sound track]
This is another romantic and
sway-able song, with all of the
best elements of disco: groovy
beat and bass line, sweeping
strings, a catchy group vocal,
and lush instrumentation. It
says "you should be dancing"
without actually saying it.

6 BROADCAST
"Valerie" — *Haha Sound*
This song features the serene
and perfect vocals of Trish
Keenan over lovely acoustic
guitar and layers of psychedelic noise that allow you to
sink into a dreamy state. The
words describe a peaceful sleepy
place, and distant open harmonies close the song like a lul-
laby from the heavens.

7 BLACK MOTH SUPER RAINBOW
"Drippy Eye" — *Dandelion Gum*
This is a song to scuba dive to.

8 SINOIA CAVES
"Through the Valley"
— *The Enchanter Persuaded*
This is the perfect sound track
for a hot-air balloon ride, or
for a ride on the back of Falkor
as he soars above the world of
Fantasia.

9 EARTH AND FIRE (NOT TO BE CONFUSED WITH EARTH, WIND AND FIRE)
"Weekend" — *Reality Fills Fantasy*
This song is off of their album
Reality Fills Fantasy, which
is one of the best and worst
albums that I own. At best,
it's like ABBA meets Kansas,
at worst, it's like ABBA meets
Kansas. (The first track off the
album is over eleven minutes
long.) But this song is pure
summer fun; it has an unex-
pected Caribbean flavor, making
it stand apart from the rest of
the songs, with a sweet reggae
beat and catchy lyrics.

HANDSOME FURS

Dan Boeckner and his wife, Alexei Perry, came up with the idea for Handsome Furs in the winter of 2006, when they wanted to take a trip to Europe, and figured the best way to do it would be to form a band and go on tour. As a result, when the enterprising duo booked their series of live dates, they hadn't written a single song—but that quickly proved not to be a problem. Boeckner, who also sings and plays guitar in Wolf Parade, and Perry, who is a writer, create minimal, raw, highly emotional music with just vocals, guitar, and a drum machine that is as anxious and unsettling as it is beautiful, and their wonderful debut album, *Plague Park*, made them card-carrying members of the indie-rock community. The following songs are particularly significant to them, they say, because they are what they listened to on their honeymoon (which they spent, appropriately enough, on tour for that first album).

1 EXUMA
"Fire in the Hole" — *Exuma II*
Uplifting, political, catchy. An aggressively weird song from a man who believed he was a voodoo priest. A sort of Bahamian Roky Erickson.

2 WIRE
"I Am the Fly" — *Chairs Missing*
Opens with guitars that sound like volleyballs being thrown against a chainlink fence. Just gets better from there.

3 NERVES
"Hanging on the Telephone" — *The Nerves* EP
Even though this band only produced a few singles, the opening four seconds of this song are better than most bands' entire recorded output.

4 IMMORTAL TECHNIQUE
"Freedom of Speech" — *Revolutionary, Vol. 2*
Required listening for anyone who has ever had to deal with a record label: "Just fuck a manager, I'll bootleg it myself...."

5 DAVID ALLEN COE
"Cocaine Carolina" — *Just Divorced/Darlin' Darlin'*
One of the only songs where the Mike Jones of country music does not mention his own name.

6 PATTI SMITH
"Rock 'n' Roll Nigger" — *Easter*
Catchy, passionate, and continues to be unbelievably harsh.

7 DOLLY PARTON
"Jolene" — *Jolene*
Desperate, pleading, and totally heartbreaking.

8 WRECKLESS ERIC
"Whole Wide World" — *Whole Wide World*
Every rock band working in the "pop format" should be forced to listen to this song. It's only two chords.

9 FORGOTTEN REBELS
"Rock & Roll's a Hard Life" — *Surfin' on Heroin*
National heroes sing a universal truth.

10 DESMOND DEKKER
"Israelites" — *Israelites: Best of Desmond Dekker*
The thing you should listen to first thing every morning. *Every* morning.

THURSTON MOORE

Sonic Youth guitarist and all-around demigod Thurston Moore is the king of MixTapes—see his book *MixTape: The Art of Cassette Culture*—so when he offered to put one together for *PLAY*, we almost hyperventilated. And then we said "Yes!" Here, a mix he calls "Songs I've Always Liked Since Getting Into Music as an Infant."

1 THE KINGSMEN

"Haunted Castle" — *The Very Best of the Kingsmen*

The instrumental B-side to "Louie, Louie." When I was a kid living in Miami, Florida, in the '60s, that record was a big hit on AM radio. My brother brought it home, and he would always play it in his room, opening the door and mouthing the words to the song. He kept saying that he and his friends *made* that record.

2 THE MONKEES

"I'm Not Your Stepping Stone" — *The Monkees: Greatest Hits*

They were a band that you could watch on TV, but that also played these completely groovy, affecting songs. I remember having this conflict: "Well, they're not the Beatles. But for us, they're bigger than the Beatles." Yes, they were a manufactured pop group from L.A. But we were the target audience—young, impressionable kids who weren't forced to process the complexities of the Beatles, because we had the Monkees. "Stepping Stone" was almost punk: It was one of the songs that was covered by all the original hardcore bands from D.C., like Minor Threat. It was anti-authoritarian.

3 TELEVISION

"Little Johnny Jewel" — *The Blow-Up*

The first 7-inch they put out. To this day it's probably one of the most important songs to me as a songwriter. It was so startling to listen to. I knew that there was this punk rock thing happening in New York at CBGB and Max's, but the first examples I heard—besides the Ramones, which was definitely energy music—were from Patti Smith. I remember getting this song, playing it, and being so taken aback by its quality because it had this really minimal, descending guitar line. The lyrics were really evocative. I thought it was such a cool thing. Like, what kind of riff is that? It had this feel of the New York streets in 1975.

4 THE YOUNGBLOODS

"Get Together" — *Get Together: The Essential Youngbloods*

There was a time in the early '70s when my mom would buy me a single from either Sears or Woolworth's once every week. I wanted "Get Together" because I'd heard it on the radio. It was the perfect stoner-hippie song for suburban kids, and it was a real influence on me because of the acoustic guitar-picking.

5 SPARKS

"This Town Ain't Big Enough for Both of Us" — *This Town Ain't Big Enough for Both of Us*

They came out of the glam scene, which I was really into, but Sparks were far more lyrically and musically radical. I liked Bowie and T. Rex, but they were so distant. The Sparks were from the U.S.A., and there was this American quality to them that I felt was very intriguing. This song has one of the best-recorded musical gunshots.

6 THE RAMONES

"Blitzkrieg Bop" — *Ramones*

At the time [in the '70s] I had been reading about the Ramones in *Rock Scene* magazine. I heard about them playing Max's Kansas City and CBGB, and then their first song, "Blitzkrieg Bop," came out pretty quickly—like they went into the studio and recorded it in a day and it came out a week later—and it was unlike anything that existed. All of a sudden, it was ripped jeans and black leather jackets and T-shirts and sneakers. And the singer was like six-foot-six. Nobody who looked like that was in a rock band, but those guys *were*. It was like the whole world changed. Everything that you fantasized about in your bedroom was realized by that band.

7 THE PATTI SMITH GROUP

"Godspeed" — *The Patti Smith Masters*

It was the B-side to her big single with Springsteen, "Because the Night." From what I gather, they did it almost as an improvisation. She had the lyrics and intoned them over this rolling song. It was what I wanted to hear from her. I liked what they were doing, but a lot of the songs by the Patti Smith Group were pretty rote rock 'n' roll, and what set them apart was how she was singing and emoting. This song had the band in this real spirited improv kind of vibe.

8 NIRVANA

"Moist Vagina" — *Singles Box Set*

Sonic Youth covered this as a B-side once. When Nirvana were working on their new record after *Nevermind*, I was in Seattle. I went with Kris and Dave to the studio where they used to rehearse, and they were playing me some songs that they had recorded. One of the songs was this one. Whatever Kurt was singing, he just broke down and started singing this chorus of "Marijuana, marijuana, marijuana," which was so nonsensical. But he was so *impassioned*, singing that word over and over again. I thought it was a brilliant way to sum up the general lunacy of being an alien youth in America at that point. I remember telling those guys, "This should be the first song on your album—that would be so rad." It ended up as a B-side. I always liked Nirvana's throwaway songs. They wrote so many songs that never got recorded, just because they weren't running a tape machine at the time. They were so prolific...but yeah, we'll never know.

THE GO! TEAM

With cheerleader-like chants, hip-hop beats, samples, guitar, piano, glockenspiel, and two drummers, six-piece U.K. band The Go! Team have created a cuckoo-crazy, ass-shaking, and unique sound. Predictably, their all-time favorite records aren't exactly middle-of-the-road.

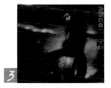

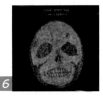

1 LEONARD COHEN

"The Story of Isaac"
— *Songs From a Room*
Leonard Cohen is an incredible
lyricist. His songs are so poetic, historical, and mysterious.
And his struggle with religion
is fascinating.

2 THE BEASTIE BOYS

"Sabotage" — *III Communication*
Not typical of Beastie Boys'
songs, but interesting because
it's a hip-hop tune but with
noise guitar and live drums.

3 TOM WAITS

"Alice" — *Alice*
Tom Waits has so many different
personas. He's the only singer
who could pull off a smoky jazz
song like this about love and
loss and make it so poignant
without being cheesy.

4 SONIC YOUTH

"Schizophrenia" — *Sister*
The perfect blueprint of a
Sonic Youth song. The guitars
are incendiary, it builds and
delivers, and the lyrics are
that beautiful mix of colorful
ambiguity and narrative.

5 SHANGRI-LAS

"Remember (Walking in the Sand)"
— *Myrmidons of Melodrama*
A song that will give you goose
bumps. The Shangri-Las are the
benchmark girl group to us.

6 BONNIE PRINCE BILLY

"I See A Darkness" — *I See A Darkness*
The album *I See A Darkness* is,
in our opinion, Bonnie Prince
Billy's masterpiece. It's a sad
but beautiful song.

7 HIJACK

"Style Wars" — *Style Wars* Single
Hijack are a bygone U.K. rap
group from the early 1990s. They
had two incredible scratch D.J.s
that spar on this tune. It's
kind of stripped-down music,
like Public Enemy.

8 BOB DYLAN

"Subterranean Homesick Blues"
— *Bringing It All Back Home*
Dylan takes the whole Woody
Guthrie-influenced phrasing to a
new level in this psychedelic
folk song. He's practically
rapping!

CHARLOTTE COOPER

THE SUBWAYS

When the Subways' debut album, *Young For Eternity,* was released in 2006, bass player Charlotte Cooper was only twenty, and she's been living the dream ever since: The Subways have appeared on *The O.C.* and *Late Night with Conan O'Brien*, opened for the Foo Fighters and The Strokes, and just finished recording their second album with Butch Vig, who worked with their idols, Nirvana. All this, and she's also engaged to Subways singer/guitarist Billy Lunn. No wonder the girl likes to dance.

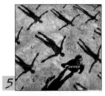
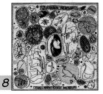

1 FRANZ FERDINAND
"Take Me Out" — *Franz Ferdinand*
Last year at the Reading festival, my two best friends came along for the day we played. We had a lot of beer then danced like idiots in the pouring rain to Franz Ferdinand. Good times.

2 NELLY FURTADO
"Maneater" — *Loose*
I've decided that I want to train for a half marathon, and this is definitely my favorite song to run (and dance!) to.

3 CANSEI DE SER SEXY
"Let's Make Love and Listen to Death From Above" — *Cansei de Ser Sexy*
This is the best song to cook to: put all the food in the oven, open the wine, and dance 'round the kitchen.

4 TAKING BACK SUNDAY
"What It Feels Like to Be a Ghost" — *Louder Now*
The tour we did last summer with Taking Back Sunday, Angels & Airwaves, and Head Automatica was amazing. TBS opened with this track every night. what a way to start a set.

5 MUSE
"Stockholm Syndrome" — *Absolution*
I could have picked any Muse track. They are the best band in the world.

6 THE VON BONDIES
"Lack of Communication" — *Lack of Communication*
The first-ever festival I went to was Reading in 2002. Billy and I came away thinking we wanted to do nothing else other than be in a band. We walked into the tent as The Von Bondies came onstage, and having never heard them before, fell in love with them.

7 NIRVANA
"About a Girl" — *Bleach*
This was the first song I learned to play on bass.

8 JOANNA NEWSOM
"Bridges and Balloons" — *The Milk-Eyed Mender*
Joanna Newsom is a new discovery for me. Now I'm trying to get hold of all of her songs.

9 PHIL COLLINS
"In the Air Tonight" — *Face Value*
This was my Dad's favorite song when I was a kid. It reminds me of bacon sandwiches on Sunday mornings.

10 THE CARDIGANS
"Lovefool" — *The First Band on the Moon*
I've kept coming back to listening to this song for years. It seems to fit with all extremes of emotion. I put it on to emphasize the good times, and smile during the bad times.

SAMANTHA RONSON

Samantha Ronson was practically born to be a music-obsessive: Her stepdad is Mick Jones of Foreigner, so family vacations were spent on the tour bus, and the likes of Yoko Ono and Keith Moon would often drop by her house for dinner. Creative talent (and drive) runs in the family—her brother is D.J./producer Mark and her twin sister is fashion designer Charlotte—and Ronson released her own songs on esteemed hip-hop label Roc-A-Fella before her D.J.ing career took off. These days, if there's a party with a velvet rope that opens only for celebrities, chances are Ronson is inside, manning the turntables. Here are her all-time favorite songs.

1 STEVIE WONDER

"I Don't Know Why" —
For Once In My Life
I envy anyone who has never felt
this way. Stevie Wonder's voice
is so beautiful and breaks so
perfectly as he sings about the
frustration he feels.

2 BLIND FAITH

"Can't Find My Way Home" —
Blind Faith
I don't know when I first heard
this song; I don't think my
memory goes back that far. I do
know that I have never made a
Top 10 mix tape without including this gem!

3 FOREIGNER

"Starrider" — *Foreigner*
I may be a little biased on
this one, because it's one of
the few Foreigner songs that my
stepfather sings lead vocals on.
But I don't care. The production
perfectly matches the mood of
the song and the lyrics paint an
incredible picture.

4 JONI MITCHELL

"A Case of You" — *Blue*
"I could drink a case of you and
still be on my feet…." Need I
say more?

5 JIMI HENDRIX

"Little Wing" — *Axis: Bold As Love*
It's so hard to put into words
why I love this song. Maybe
because it's so short. But I
just do.

6 ANI DIFRANCO

"You Had Time" — *Out of Range*
The other side of love.

7 THE TEMPTATIONS

"I Wish It Would Rain" —
I Wish It Would Rain
"Raindrops will hide the tear-
drops…." I usually hate when
artists rhyme a word with the
same word, because it's not really rhyming. However, in this
case it seems so perfect and innocent that it doesn't matter.

8 DON HENLEY
(FEATURING AXL ROSE)

"I Will Not Go Quietly" — *The End
of the Innocence*
You can't live in L.A. and not
relate to this song.

9 THE BEATLES

"For No One" — *Revolver*
Hard to choose a favorite from
their catalogue. *Revolver* is
probably my favorite album though.

10 DAMIEN RICE

"Cannonball" — *O*
I judged this album by its cover
and was rewarded—so fuck that
theory! I think I listened to
this song more than twenty times
in a row when I first heard it:
Traffic, heartbreak, and this
song made for a great combination. It's such a beautifully
written love song. Timeless and
painful.

SARAH LEWITINN

ULTRAGRRRL

Sarah Lewitinn, a.k.a. Ultragrrrl, has proven that being a passionate fan can really take you places. By championing bands—including My Chemical Romance, Interpol, Franz Ferdinand, and the Killers— on her eponymous music blog, she became an influential figure on the New York music scene, and, after putting in time as a *Spin* magazine staffer, has written two music books, *The Pocket D.J.* and *Pocket Karaoke*. She also D.J.s a weekly party in New York, and still finds time to run her own record label, Island Records subsidiary Stolen Transmission. Phew! These, she says, are "the songs that define who I am today."

1 ECHO & THE BUNNYMEN
"The Cutter" — *Porcupine*

I remember the first time I heard this song—I was fifteen and really getting into a compilation collection called *New Wave Hits of the '80s* that my brother Lawrence had—and then I listened to it over and over again. Once, I even went to a party at my friend Sydney's house and instead of hanging out and drinking with everyone else, I sat in her room playing this on repeat and dancing around her bedroom...alone.

2 ARCADE FIRE
"Rebellion (Lies)" — *Funeral*

The excitement that rushes through me when I listen to this song is immeasurable. I just picture having someone I'm excited about but at the same time ashamed of. It's a romantic notion, and I'm fairly certain that isn't what this song is about, but that's how it makes me feel. The bass drum pulsates like my heart when I see someone I love.

3 PLACEBO
"36 Degrees" — *Placebo*

I got into Placebo after reading an interview they did for *Select* magazine. It featured Brian Molko on the cover with his shirt spread open to reveal his chest and the headline "HELLO BOYS." He looked exactly like me! It was basically love at first sight, and made me realize I was maybe a narcissist. Anyway, this song made me so excited about life.

4 THE OOHLAS
"The Rapid" — *Best Stop Pop*

It might seem lame for me to pick a song from my own label for this mix tape, but "The Rapid" is what made me go from an Oohlas fan to an Oohlas obsessive. I had a couple of arguments with someone about putting this song on their album, but I couldn't handle the idea of people not hearing it!

5 INTERPOL
"Not Even Jail" — *Antics*

I think that Paul Banks is one of the finest lyricists ever. He's poetic and underrated as a wordsmith. If he wasn't writing songs, he'd be in some café in Paris drinking absinthe, fighting off a heroin addiction, and having a gay love affair just like Arthur Rimbaud.

6 THE SMITHS
"Rubber Ring" — *Louder than Bombs*

I don't think I would've made it through life this far if it wasn't for The Smiths. I had really strict parents, and as a teenager, I wasn't allowed to hang out with friends outside of school. The only way I could socialize was by working, so I would work on the sets for school plays or get internships in the city, and listen to The Smiths whenever I was alone so I would feel less lonely.

7 RADIOHEAD
"Let Down" — *OK Computer*

I remember spooning with my boombox when I was eighteen while listening to "Let Down" because I wanted to be closer to the music. Radiohead meant the world to me from the ages of seventeen through twenty-two. I didn't want to live without them. This is the best song they'll ever write, I think.

8 THE KILLERS
"Midnight Show" — *Hot Fuss*

I heard this song for the first time in 2003 when I saw them play at Don Hill's for CMJ. The second they played it, I knew that, poof, they would be big. I think this song is so naughty and spastic. Not long after, my best friend Karen and I went to London when they were playing a handful of shows there. Each night we'd stand up front at small clubs and when this song would get played, my heart would jump.

9 HOLE
"Credit in the Straight World" — *Live Through This*

I was a very conservative kid who wanted nothing more than to rebel. The punk rock lifestyle was so appealing and dirty and wrong, and I just wanted to be a part of it. Courtney Love isn't the best singer, but she's the best protagonist.

10 MUSE
"Apocalypse Please" — *Absolution*

I've been a huge fan of Muse since 1999, when my friend Marc Spitz handed me their album *Showbiz* and said, "I heard this sounds like Radiohead." I finally was able to give *OK Computer* a much needed rest after listening to it three times a day, and put something else in my player.

11 NIRVANA
"Lithium" — *Nevermind*

Nirvana defined my teenhood. I was full of angst. My parents didn't understand me and were constantly fighting with me and each other, and I felt really lost. I turned to Nirvana because I thought that Kurt *understood* me. "Lithium" is the best song by Nirvana in my opinion.

12 JOY DIVISION
"Love Will Tear Us Apart" — *Substance*

The most fond memories of my life—ever—occurred when I was making out with a boy on the dance floor while this song was playing. It's happened with about five boys.

ROCK POSTERS MAY HAVE EXPERIENCED
THEIR HEYDAY IN THE HEADY PSYCHEDELIC
'60S, BUT THEY'VE CONTINUED TO
BE A THRIVING (AND INCREASINGLY
COLLECTIBLE) ART FORM. THEY OFFER YET
ANOTHER VISUAL DIMENSION (BEYOND CD
SLEEVES, VIDEOS, AND BAND WEB SITES)
TO THE MUSIC WE LOVE, AND OFTEN,
BECAUSE THEY ARE MADE WITH SUCH
CREATIVE FREEDOM, THEY BECOME JUST AS
MEMORABLE AS THE SHOWS THEMSELVES.
UNBURDENED BY THE LIMITATIONS OF TIME,
SPACE, AND LOGIC, WE HAD A FEW TALENTED
ILLUSTRATORS, FASHION DESIGNERS, AND
ARTISTICALLY INCLINED MUSICIANS DREAM
UP THEIR ULTIMATE CONCERT BILLS.

POSTE

CHAPTER 4

RS

Wayne Coyne
THE FLAMING LIPS

If any band is going to be the first to play on Mars, it's got to be the Flaming Lips. They've already been making planet Earth a better place with their mind-blowing psych-rock since 1983, and whether it's arriving onstage in a giant plastic bubble, shooting confetti guns into the audience, or drenching himself in fake blood, wild-haired front man Wayne Coyne knows what it takes to put on an epic show. And so it's little surprise that Coyne's poster stars his own band—along with fellow Oklahoma City weirdo-rockers Stardeath and White Dwarfs—because for this band, playing on Mars actually seems…feasible. In fact, one suspects that the Lips have already been talking to aliens in preparation. But really, Wayne, do we have to wait until 2024?

Faris Badwan
THE HORRORS

The Horrors look like they sprang from the imagination of Tim Burton and sound like goth-garage-rock crypt-keepers. Ever since they first met in the Junk Club—run by keyboard player Spider Webb in the basement of a decaying Victorian hotel in England's Southend—the black-clad quintet have been scaring up obsessed acolytes the world over. For his poster, front man Faris Badwan gives us a glimpse into the M.C. Escher-like labyrinth of his brain, and reveals his love for (and ability to correctly spell!) German experimental noise-makers Einsturzende Neubauten (whose name, incidentally, translates as "buildings that are collapsing"), as well as defunct New York No Wave band DNA, and abrasively dissonant California freak-punk pioneers Flipper. Sounds like a headache well worth having.

Patience, Alana & John
THE GRATES

The Grates come from the land of Oz—well, Australia—and while they may humbly describe themselves as "three best friends who play music for 30 min. to 1 hr.," they are truly much, much more. Not only do Patience Hodgson, Alana Skyring, and John Patterson make some of the happiest music (and put on some of the giddiest shows) we know, it turns out that tunes aren't their only area of expertise: They also design their own album artwork and clothing. Making this poster, then, was a snap. And it's a thing of beauty. Who wouldn't want to see some amazing bands in a place called Ghost Island? Spooky wonderfulness.

Maya Wild
THE BOOS

British artist and art director Maya Wild is one half of illustration team the Boos. She's known for her fabulous drawings of rock stars from M.I.A. to Dizzee Rascal to Joni Mitchell, and her work has appeared in the world's coolest magazines (including *NYLON*, naturally) as well as major exhibitions in Tokyo, Paris, and London. "At my fantasy concert," she says, "I would go backstage and meet Prince—my first true musical love—and it would be the beginning of a lifelong friendship."

CAFE DE PARIS .9TH JUNE. 8—LATE

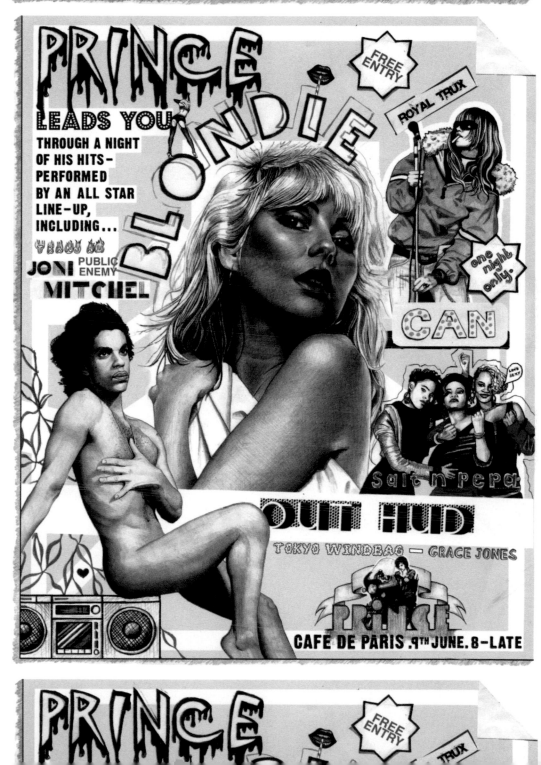

PRINCE

FREE ENTRY

ROYAL TRUX

LEADS YOU

BLONDIE

THROUGH A NIGHT
OF HIS HITS—
PERFORMED
BY AN ALL STAR
LINE—UP,
INCLUDING...

TRACY AM

JONI MITCHEL

PUBLIC ENEMY

one night only.

CAN

Salt 'n' Pepa

OUT HUD

TOKYO WINDBAG — GRACE JONES

CAFE DE PARIS .9TH JUNE. 8—LATE

PRINCE

FREE ENTRY

TRUX

Steve Aoki
DIM MAK

Steve Aoki seems to be so many places at the same time, a casual observer might think that he's had himself cloned. In addition to running Dim Mak Records, the label he founded in L.A. in 1996 (which has released music by Klaxons, Mystery Jets, Foreign Born, The Deadly Syndrome, The Icarus Line, Bloc Party, and Whitey, among many others), the inveterate nightclubber is constantly bouncing back and forth from coast to coast D.J.ing at parties, fashion shows, and gigs. He also found time to make an album of his own—*Pillowface and His Airplane Chronicles* (2007)—and expand Dim Mak into a clothing line. For his poster—designed by Dim Mak's party-flyer creators—he pulled together all of his favorite artists, most of whom he's worked with at some point, for a gigantic Dim Mak blowout.

Rachel & Alison
MOOKA KINNEY

Rachel Antonoff and Alison Lewis are the duo behind cute and whimsical clothing line Mooka Kinney. With vintage-fabric patterns, playful designs, and the cutest buttons (ponies! ducks!) you've seen since that romper you wore when you were six, it's little surprise that Mooka Kinney dresses have found their ways onto so many musicians and music-lovers. They chose to take an unconventional approach to their poster, making it into more of a collage. Here's what they have to say about it:

"Some of the acts on our fantasy lineup were chosen because they are musicians that we are already proud to dress: Au Revoir Simone, Jenny Lewis, Tilly and the Wall, The Format, Steel Train, Scarlett Johansson. The rest are musicians we idolize and who inspire our dresses: Joanna Newsom, Nancy Sinatra, Becky Stark of Lavender Diamond, El Perro Del Mar, Patsy Cline, Dolly Parton, Buffy Sainte-Marie, Mama Cass, Joni Mitchell, Marianne Faithfull, Yoko Ono, The Shangri-Las, and Grace Slick. Many of these inspirations are from the '50s and '60s and a lot of the pictures are from album covers from our own vinyl collections, or objects that are in our studio that we use for inspiration! If we could have our fantasy show anywhere, it would be at the Winterland Ballroom. It was an ice skating rink that [legendary rock promoter] Bill Graham made into a venue; the first show there was Jefferson Airplane and it was where *The Last Waltz* was filmed. Sadly, it closed down."

Eddie Argos
ART BRUT

Clearly, Art Brut front man Eddie Argos is not a great artist. But he'd be the first to admit it, we're sure—as so many of the band's songs (such as "Formed a Band" or "Bang Bang Rock & Roll") emphasize enthusiasm over skill. And so it follows that while his poster itself may be somewhat rudimentary, it promises something quite spectacular: a show starring Scottish pre-Franz Ferdinand cult band the Yummy Fur, odd-bod folk-rock outfit the Mountain Goats, and downtown NYC anti-folk funny guy Jeffrey Lewis. The venue, Dublin Castle, is a dingy-but-legendary pub in London that, despite smelling like sweat and vomit, has hosted some of the most phenomenal bands in history. Pints are cheap there too.

JD Samson
LE TIGRE & MEN

JD Samson has certainly taken an adventurous career path: she's logged time as a feminist electropunk pioneer in Le Tigre (she worked as the band's projectionist before replacing original member Sadie Benning in 2000), as well as playing in the New England Roses, and Peaches' live band, the Herms. The Sarah Lawrence graduate has also collaborated with Junior Senior, appeared in John Cameron Mitchell's film *Shortbus*, published a lesbian calendar with photographer Cass Bird, and now has a cool producing, remixing, and D.J.ing project, Men, with fellow Le Tigre member Johanna Fateman. Her poster is not only for a show by ladies and for ladies, it also reveals a penchant for percussion. In addition to her headliners, she has performance artist and drummer Ubaka Hill, ESG drummer Valerie Scroggins, ten-piece all-girl British drumming band Leopard Leg, and legendary Boredoms drummer Yoshimi. Oh, and Missy Elliott. Eclectic and statement-making—who would expect anything less?

FOR SOME IT'S "I WISH I WAS DRINKING ABSINTHE IN A DUNGEON WITH MARILYN MANSON"; FOR OTHERS "I OWN EVERY BELLE & SEBASTIAN RECORD. CUDDLE ME." OFTEN THE STATEMENTS AREN'T QUITE SO EXTREME, BUT MANY OF US LITERALLY WEAR THE MUSIC WE LOVE ON OUR SLEEVES. WHAT WE LISTEN TO TENDS TO FILTER DOWN TO WHAT WE WEAR (EVEN IF IT'S JUST A HAIRCUT OR A PAIR OF CHUCKS) AND OVER THE YEARS, ROCK 'N' ROLL HAS SPAWNED MANY FASHION "TRIBES"—TEDDY BOYS, MODS, PUNKS, GOTHS, EMO-KIDS, MET-AL-HEADS, NEW RAVERS, AND THE LIST GOES ON AND ON—BECAUSE MUSIC, LIKE PERSONAL STYLE, DEFINES WHO WE ARE, AND DRAWS US TOGETHER WITH LIKE-MINDED STRANGERS. IT'S ABOUT BOTH SELF-EXPRESSION AND IDENTIFI-CATION; ABOUT BEING YOURSELF AND BEING A PART OF SOMETHING BIGGER.

CHAPTER **5**

FAN
STYLE

UFFIE

TALES OF THE JACKALOPE FESTIVAL
NORFOLK. UK

LINEUP : DIZZEE RASCAL, THE FALL, 2 MANY DJS, ESG, CHROMEO, FUCKED UP, THE HOURS, UFFIE AND FEADZ, CHRIS CUNNINGHAM, FRIENDLY FIRES, LIGHTSPEED CHAMPION, KISSY SELL OUT, OX.EAGLE.LION.MAN

ADAM

WHO IS YOUR MUSIC STYLE ICON?

Interpol

SYBILLA

**WHAT'S THE MOST ESSENTIAL THING
TO BRING TO A FESTIVAL?**
Poppers
and a fleecy
blanket

WHO IS YOUR MUSIC STYLE ICON?
Marilyn
Manson

LOUISE

WHO IS YOUR MUSIC STYLE ICON?
Sybilla

KATIE

**WHAT'S THE MOST
ESSENTIAL THING TO
BRING TO A FESTIVAL?**

A picnic

**WHO IS YOUR MUSIC
STYLE ICON?**

Kate
Moss

MCCARREN PARK POOL — BROOKLYN, NY

LINEUP : TED LEO AND THE PHARMACISTS, THE THERMALS, BIRDS OF AVALON

ERICA

WHO IS YOUR MUSIC STYLE ICON:

Tracy and
the Plastics

BRANDI

<u>MOST IMPORTANT THING TO
BRING TO A SHOW:</u>

Tissues,
'cause you
know the
bathroom
is always
out!

REBBECA

**MOST IMPORTANT THING TO BRING
TO A MUSIC FESTIVAL?**

Sunglasses
and wallet

**MOST IMPORTANT THING TO
BRING TO A MUSIC FESTIVAL?**

Dancing
shoes

CELIA

WHO IS YOUR MUSIC STYLE ICON?

OK Go!

MCCARREN PARK POOL — BROOKLYN, NY

LINEUP: GHOSTLAND OBSERVATORY, THE RUB, THE BALTIMORE BASS CONNECTION, THE COOL KIDS, KID SISTER, BETTY BLACK, PASE ROCK, YACHT

JENIFER

WHO IS YOUR MUSIC STYLE ICON?

M.I.A.

WHO IS YOUR MUSIC STYLE ICON?

The music I listen to as I'm getting ready can set the tone for how vamp, flashy, overstated, or casual I might want to dress on that occasion.

NINA

SAMANTHA

WHAT'S THE MOST
ESSENTIAL THING TO
BRING TO A MUSIC
FESTIVAL?

Power

SARAH

MAGGIE

Myself

STUDIO B
BROOKLYN, NY
LINEUP : STANDING NUDES, MGMT, ARTANKER CONVOY

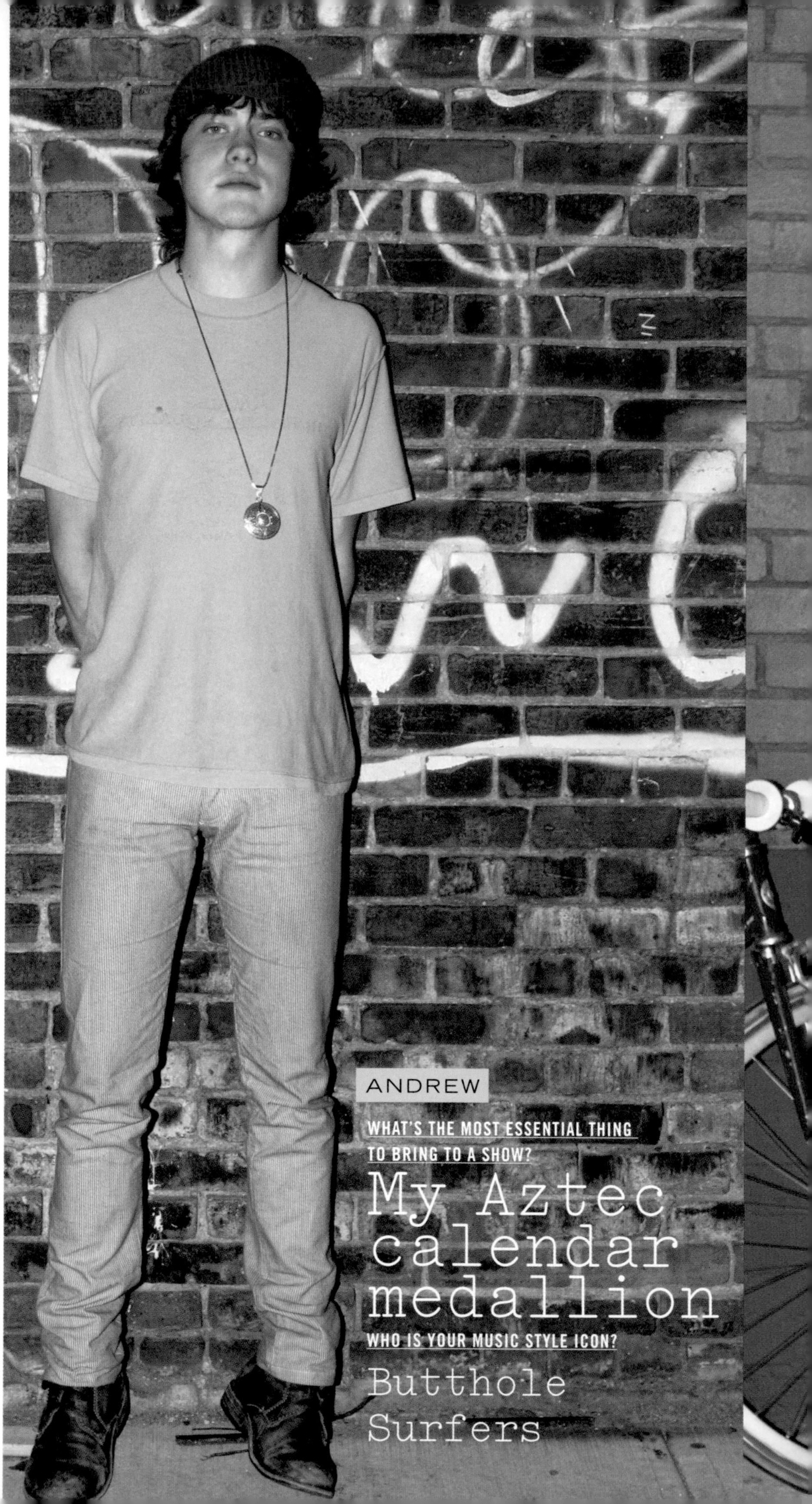

ANDREW

WHAT'S THE MOST ESSENTIAL THING TO BRING TO A SHOW?

My Aztec calendar medallion

WHO IS YOUR MUSIC STYLE ICON?

Butthole Surfers

TIM

WHO IS YOUR MUSIC STYLE ICON?

Miles
Davis

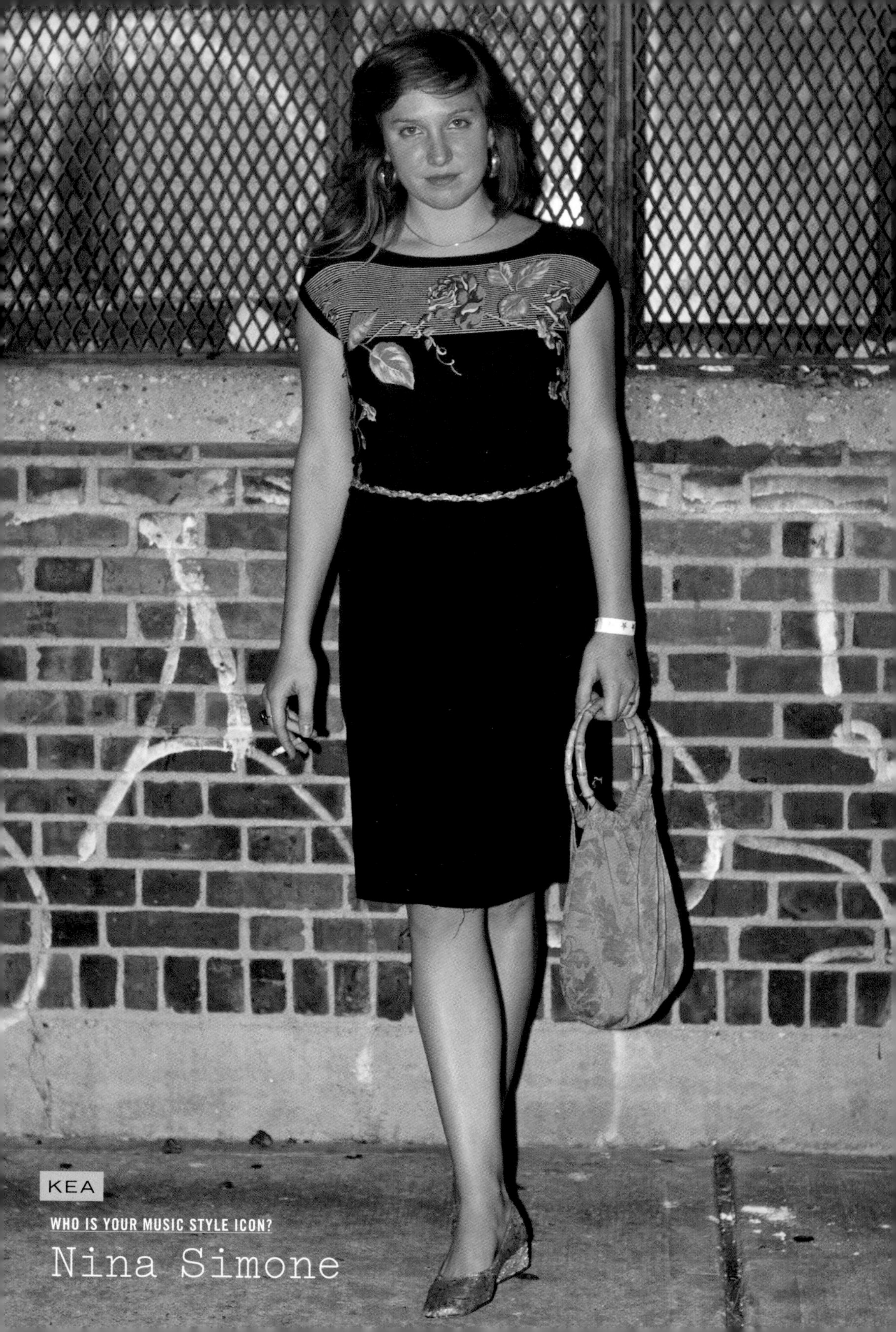

KEA

WHO IS YOUR MUSIC STYLE ICON?

Nina Simone

CINESPACE
LOS ANGELES, CA

LINEUP : DJ STEVE AOKI, KID MILLIONAIRE

RHIANNON

WHAT'S THE MOST ESSENTIAL THING TO BRING TO A SHOW?

Comfortable shoes

JENNIFER

WHO IS YOUR MUSIC STYLE ICON?

Steve Aoki

JEANEEN

WHAT'S THE MOST ESSENTIAL THING TO BRING TO A SHOW?

Dancing
shoes, camera
and fake i.d.

LINEUP : ARCTIC MONKEYS, KASABIAN, THE FRATELLIS, BLOC PARTY, AMY WINEHOUSE, THE KILLERS, THE KOOKS, LILY ALLEN, THE PIPETTES, THE WHO, KAISER CHIEFS, BJÖRK, ARCADE FIRE, SUPER FURRY ANIMALS , BRIGHT EYES, MODEST MOUSE, IGGY AND THE STOOGES, BABYSHAMBLES, KLAXONS, CSS, THE LONG BLONDES, M.I.A., KATE NASH, THE GO! TEAM, HOT CHIP, THE HOLD STEADY, TOKYO POLICE CLUB, PATRICK WOLF, THE GOSSIP

WHAT'S THE MOST ESSENTIAL THING TO
BRING TO A SHOW?

Wellingtons

METTE

WHAT'S THE MOST ESSENTIAL THING TO BRING TO A FESTIVAL?

Hand sanitizer

WHO IS YOUR MUSIC STYLE ICON?

Courtney Love

KATE

WHO IS YOUR MUSIC STYLE ICON?

Natasha Khan from Bat for Lashes

WHO IS YOUR MUSIC STYLE ICON?

Debbie
Harry

CONEY ISLAND ROCKABILLY FESTIVAL

BROOKLYN, NY

LINEUP : THE HOLY ROLLER SIDESHOW AND BURLESQUE REVUE, SASQUATCH AND THE SICK-A-BILLYS, FURY 3, TOMBSTONE BRAWLERS, JASON JAMES AND THE BAY STATE HOUSE , ERS, FISHERMAN ORCHESTRA, SEAN KERSHAW AND THE NEW JACK RAMBLERS

WHO IS YOUR MUSIC STYLE ICON?

Bad Brains

WHO IS YOUR MUSIC STYLE ICON?

Animal from
the Muppets

GRAMERCY THEATRE
NEW YORK, NY
LINEUP : TWO GALLANTS, SONGS FOR MOMS

ENRICA

WHAT'S THE MOST ESSENTIAL THING TO BRING TO A SHOW?

My flask! And good dancing shoes.

WHO IS YOUR MUSIC STYLE ICON?

Debbie Harry

**AUSTIN CITY LIMITS FESTIVAL
AUSTIN, TX**

LINEUP : BOB DYLAN & HIS BAND, BJÖRK, THE KILLERS, WILCO, ARCADE FIRE, MUSE, MY MORNING JACKET, QUEENS OF THE STONE AGE, BLOC PARTY, ARCTIC MONKEYS, SPOON, THE DECEMBERISTS, REGINA SPEKTOR, KAISER CHIEFS, LCD SOUNDSYSTEM, M.I.A., CLAP YOUR HANDS SAY YEAH, PETER BJORN AND JOHN, COLD WAR KIDS, BLONDE REDHEAD, DR. DOG , THE NATIONAL

REGINA

David Bowie

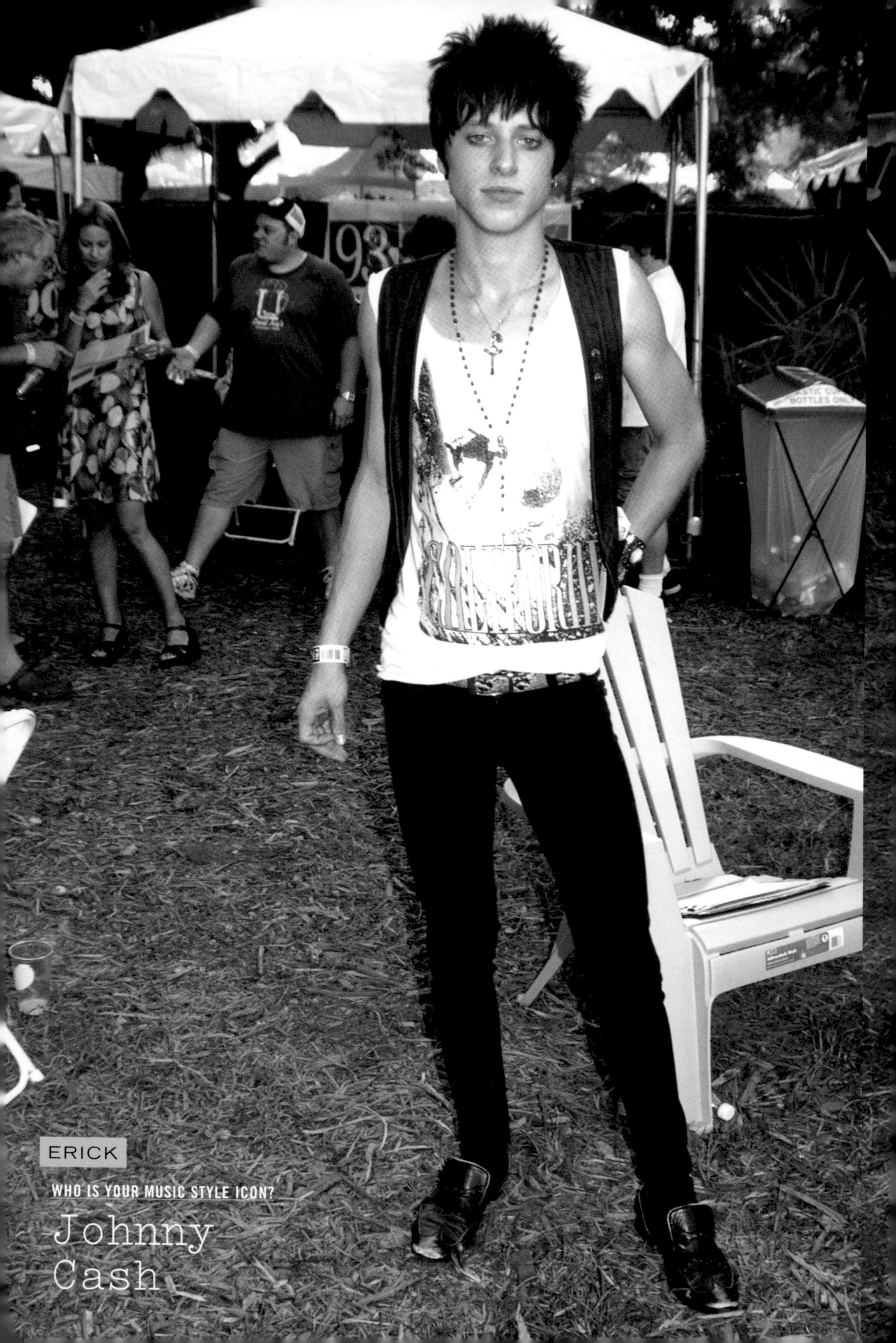

ERICK

WHO IS YOUR MUSIC STYLE ICON?

Johnny
Cash

ANNIE

COURTNEY

WHO IS YOUR MUSIC STYLE ICON?

Nico

ELIZABETH

WHO IS YOUR MUSIC STYLE ICON?

Gwen Stefani

**WHO IS YOUR MUSIC
STYLE ICON?**

The
Rolling
Stones

JESSICA

WHO IS YOUR MUSIC STYLE ICON?

Bob Marley

RANDALL'S ISLAND
NEW YORK, NY

LINEUP : ARCADE FIRE, LCD SOUNDSYSTEM, LES SAVY FAV, BLONDE REDHEAD, WILD LIGHT

KELLY

**WHO IS YOUR MUSIC
STYLE ICON?**

Kelis

KATE

**WHAT'S THE MOST ESSENTIAL
THING TO BRING TO A SHOW?**

Anything but
your camera

WHO IS YOUR MUSIC STYLE ICON?

Dolly
Parton

ROSE

**WHAT'S THE MOST ESSENTIAL
THING TO BRING TO A SHOW?**

A good
presence

WHO IS YOUR MUSIC STYLE ICON?

Iggy Pop

ERIN

WHO IS YOUR MUSIC STYLE ICON?

I love Nicole Richie's style, although she's no artist.

WILLIAMSBURG HALL OF MUSIC
BROOKLYN, NY

LINEUP : BORIS, DAMON & NAOMI, MICHIO KURIHARA

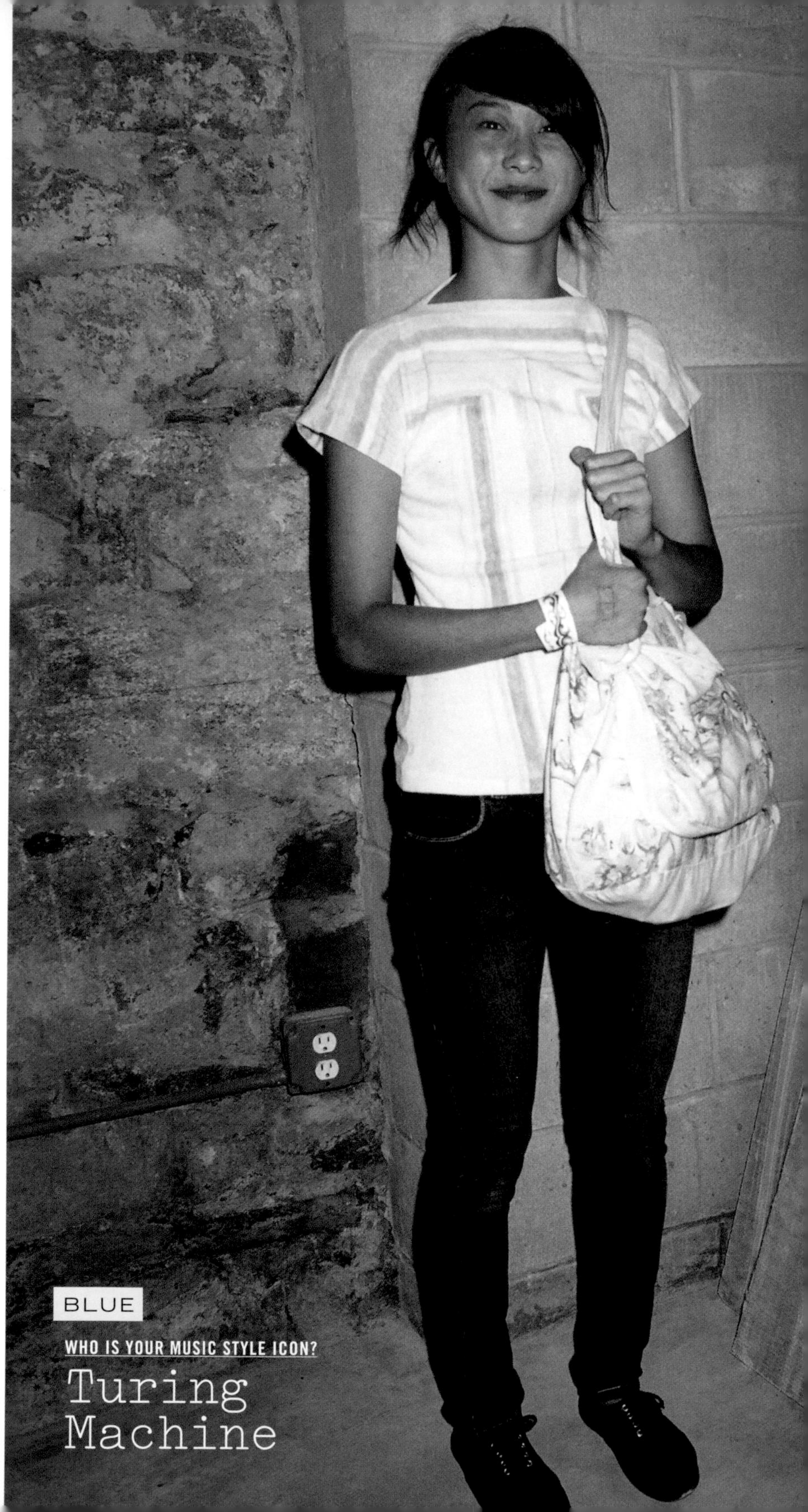

BLUE

WHO IS YOUR MUSIC STYLE ICON?

Turing Machine

WHO IS YOUR MUSIC STYLE ICON?

Birds of Avalon

MARIATI

WHAT'S THE MOST ESSENTIAL THING TO BRING TO A SHOW?

A good vibe

WHO IS YOUR MUSIC STYLE ICON?

The Captain
(japan)

WHO IS YOUR MUSIC
STYLE ICON?

Revenge

OZZFEST

HOLMDEL,NJ

LINEUP : OZZY OSBOURNE, LAMB OF GOD, STATIC-X, LORDI, HATEBREED, BEHEMOTH, DEVILDRIVER, NILE, ANKLA, THE SHOWDOWN , 3 INCHES OF BLOOD, IN THIS MOMENT, BLACK TIDE

ELIZABETH

WHAT'S THE MOST ESSENTIAL THING TO BRING TO A FESTIVAL?

I'd say either energy, or a smile. Things are so much more enjoyable with these two things.

WHO IS YOUR MUSIC STYLE ICON?

Avenged

JESSICA

WHO IS YOUR MUSIC STYLE ICON?

DevilDriver

WILLIAMSBURG HALL OF MUSIC

BROOKLYN, NY

LINEUP : THURSTON MOORE

MAYA

WHO IS YOUR MUSIC STYLE ICON?

My Bloody
Valentine

JULIE

Blonde
Redhead

JENNIE

WHO IS YOUR MUSIC STYLE ICON?
Yeah Yeah
Yeahs

WHO IS YOUR MUSIC STYLE ICON?

Os Mutantes

WHO IS YOUR MUSIC STYLE ICON?

Black Flag

GRACE

WHAT'S THE MOST ESSENTIAL THING TO BRING TO A SHOW?

Ear Plugs

WHO IS YOUR MUSIC STYLE ICON?

Jenny Lewis

MELISSA

WHAT'S THE MOST ESSENTIAL THING TO BRING TO A SHOW?

Shoes!!

WHO IS YOUR MUSIC STYLE ICON?

Neil Young

CHAPTER **6**

URCES

SHOPPING LIST

MANHATTAN

A-1 RECORDS
439 E. 6th Street
212-473-2870

ACADEMY RECORDS
12 W. 18th Street
212-242-3000

ACCIDENTAL CDS, RECORDS, AND TAPES
131 Avenue A
212-995-2224

AUDIO FORCE
630 Ninth Avenue
212-262-1717

BLEECKER STREET RECORDS
239 Bleecker Street
212-255-7899
www.bleeckerstreetrecords.com

CAKE SHOP
152 Ludlow Street
212-253-0036
www.cake-shop.com

EAST VILLAGE MUSIC STORE
85 E. 4th Street
212-979-8222
www.evmnyc.com

ETHEREA
66 Avenue A
212-358-1126
www.estetherea.net

FAT BEATS
406 Sixth Avenue
212-673-3883

FINYL VINYL
204 E. 6th Street
212-533-8007

FIRST FLIGHT MUSIC
174 First Avenue
212-539-1383
www.firstflightmusic.com

GRYPHON RECORD SHOPS
233 W. 72nd Street
212-874-1588

GUITAR CENTER MANHATTAN
25 W. 14th Street
212-463-7500
www.guitarcenter.com

GUITAR MAN
147 Orchard Street
212-475-5150
www.guitarmannyc.com

HARLEM RECORD SHACK
274 W. 125th Street
212-866-1600
www.harlemrecordshack.com

LUDLOW GUITARS
164 Ludlow Street
212-353-1775

MONDO KIM'S
6 St. Marks Place
212-598-9985
www.mondokims.com

NYCD
325 W. 38th Street
212-244-3460
www.nycd-online.com

OTHER MUSIC
15 E. 4th Street
212-477-8150
www.othermusic.com

REBEL REBEL
319 Bleecker Street
212-989-0770

ROCKET SCIENTIST
43 Carmine Street
212-242-0066

SATELLITE
259 Bowery
212-995-1744

THE SOUND LIBRARY
214 Avenue A
212-598-9302

ST. MARKS SOUNDS
20 St. Marks Place
212-677-3444

VIRGIN MEGASTORE
52 E. 14th Street
212-598-4666
www.virginmegamagazine.com

BROOKLYN

EARWAX RECORDS
218 Bedford Avenue
718-486-3771

HALCYON
57 Pearl Street
718-260-9299
www.halcyonline.com

MUSIC MATTERS
413 7th Avenue
718-369-7087

THING
1001 Manhattan Avenue
718-349-8234

LOS ANGELES

AMOEBA
6400 Sunset Boulevard
323-245-6400
www.amoeba.com

DIETZ BROTHERS MUSIC
240 S. Sepulveda Blvd. Ste B
310-379-6799

FANTASTIC MUSICAL INSTRUMENTS
1399 N. Lake Avenue
626-794-7554
www.gotofmi.com

HEAR MUSIC
1429 3rd Street
310-319-9527
www.hearmusic.com

INTERNATIONAL HOUSE OF MUSIC
339 S. BROADWAY
213-628-9161

MCCABE'S GUITAR SHOP
3101 Pico Boulevard
310-828-4497
www.mccabes.com

RECORD SURPLUS
11609 W. Pico Boulevard
310-478-4217
www.recordsurplusla.com

SAM ASH MUSIC STORE
7360 W. Sunset Boulevard
323-850-1050
www.samashmusic.com

TRUETONE MUSIC
714 Santa Monica Boulevard
310-393-8232
www.truetonemusic.com

VIRGIN RECORDS MEGASTORE
8000 Sunset Boulevard
323-650-8666
www.virginmegamagazine.com

WEST LA MUSIC
3501 Cahuenga Boulevard
West
323-845-1145
www.westlamusic.com

CHICAGO

ANDY'S MUSICAL INSTRUMENTS
2300 W. Belmont Avenue
773-868-1234
www.andysmusic.com

AVENUE N GUITARS
1823 W. North Avenue
773-252-5580

BEVERLY RARE RECORD SHOP
11612 S. Western Avenue
773-779-0066
www.beverlyrecords.com

C&G MUSIC
3125 W. 26th Street
773-847-3402

CHICAGO MUSIC EXCHANGE
3316 N. Lincoln Avenue
773-525-7773
www.chicagomusic
exchange.com

COOP'S RECORDS
1613 W. 87th Street
773-238-2566

DAVE'S RECORDS
2604 N. Clark Street
773-929-6325

DEADWAX RECORDS
3819 N. Lincoln Avenue
773-529-1932

DISCUS CD EXCHANGE
2935 N. Broadway Street
773-868-0952

DUSTY GROOVE AMERICA
1120 N. Ashland Avenue
773-342-5800

GAND MUSIC AND SOUND
780 W. Frontage Road
847-446-GAND

GEORGE'S MUSIC ROOM
5700 S. Cicero Avenue
773-767-4676

GROOVIN HIGH INC.
1047 W. Belmont Avenue
773-476-6846

HARD BOILED RECORDS AND VIDEO
2010 W. Roscoe Street
773-755-2619

HYDE PARK RECORDS
1377 E. 53rd Street
773-288-6588

LAURIE'S PLANET OF SOUND
4639 N. Lincoln Avenue
773-271-3569
www.lauriesplanetof
sound.com

MAKE'N MUSIC
1455 W. Hubbard Street
312-455-1970

MR. PEABODY RECORDS
11832 S. Western Avenue
773-881-9299
www.mrpeabodyrecords.com

MUSIC EXPERIENCE
1959 1/2 E. 73rd Street
773-493-0154
www.amusicexperience.com

OLD SCHOOL RECORDS
7446 Madison Street
708-366-7588
www.theoldschoolrecords.com

PERMANENT RECORDS
1914 W. Chicago Avenue
773-278-1744
www.ermanentrecordschicago.
com

RECORD DUGOUT USED RECORDS
6055 W. 63rd Street
773-586-1206

REVOLVER RECORD STORE
1524 W. 18th Street
312-226-4211

TOMMY'S GUITARS & COLLECTIBLES
2548 W. Chicago Avenue
773-486-6768
www.tommysguitars.com

WAX ADDICT
1014 N. Ashland Avenue
773-772-9930
www.waxaddict.com

LONDON

ABC MUSIC
20 Ridgway
020 8739 0202
www.abcmusic.co.uk

ANDY'S DRUM CENTRE
27 Denmark Place
Basement
020 7836 4522

ASM MUSIC
318A Kennington Road
020 7735 1932
www.asmmusic.co.uk

BARBICAN CHIMES MUSIC SHOP
Cromwell Tower
Silk Street
020 7588 9242
www.chimesmusic.com/barbican

CHAPPELL OF BOND STREET
152-160 Wardour Street
020 7432 4400
www.chappellofbondstreet.
co.uk

CHEAPO CHEAPO RECORDS
53 Rupert Street
020 7437 8272

CLERKENWELL MUSIC
27 Exmouth Market
020 7833 9757
www.clerkenwellmusic.co.uk

DIVISION ONE

36 Hanway Street
020 7637 7734
www.divisionone.co.uk

GRAHAM PARKER

13 Sandrock Road
020 8694 2770
www.gparker.co.uk

GUITAR CLASSICS

38 Webb's Road
020 7738 2974
www.guitar-classics.co.uk

HANK'S GUITAR SHOP

24 Denmark Street
020 7379 1139
www.hanksguitarshop.com

HMV

150 Oxford Street
0845 602 7800
360 Oxford Street
0845 602 7802
www.hmv.co.uk

HONEST JONS

278 Portobello Road
020 8969 9822
www.honestjons.com

INTOXICA

231 Portobello Road
020 7229 8010
www.intoxica.co.uk

LONDON BASS SELLER

22 Denmark Street
020 7240 3483

LONDON MUSIC LTD

120 Broughton Road
020 7751 0222
www.london-music.co.uk

MINUS ZERO RECORDS

2 Blenheim Crescent
(020) 7229 5424
www.minuszerorecords.com

MUSIC AND VIDEO EXCHANGE

38-40 Notting Hill Gate
020 7243 8573
www.mveshops.co.uk

PHONICA RECORDS

51 Poland Street
020 7025 6070
www.phonicarecords.co.uk

RECKLESS RECORDS

26/30 Berwick Street
020 7434 3362
www.reckless.co.uk

ROSE MORRIS MUSICAL INSTRUMENTS

10 Denmark Street
020 7836 0991
www.rosemorris.com

ROUGH TRADE

130 Talbot Road
020 7229 8541
www.roughtrade.com

VIRGIN RECORD MEGASTORE

14 - 16 , Oxford Street
020 7631 1234
www.virginmega.co.uk

CREDITS

TITLE PAGE: Madonna: Courtesy of Everett Collection
TABLE OF CONTENTS: Debbie Harry: Courtesy of Retna
PAGE 6: Photograph by Marvin Scott Jarrett
PAGE 9: Photograph by Stephen Walker
PAGE 12: Marianne Faithfull: Courtesy of Everett Collection
PAGE 13: Lancôme Color Design Lipstick in Pale Lip. *Marianne Faithfull*: Courtesy of Universal Music Enterprises. *Faithfull: An Autobiography*: Courtesy of Cooper Square Press. *Girl On A Motorcycle*: Courtesy of Ares Production; Trench by Uniqlo and scarf by Aruliden for Volkswagen eos.
PAGE 14: Nico: Courtesy of Everett Collection. *The Velvet Underground & Nico*: Courtesy of Universal Music Enterprises. *Chelsea Girl*: Courtesy of Universal Music Enterprises. Cover of *Nico, Songs They Never Play on the Radio* by James Young: Published by Bloomsbury Publishing PLC, 1992.
PAGE 15: Moe Tucker: Courtesy of Everett Collection. *The Velvet Underground*: Courtesy of Universal Music Enterprises. *Up-tight: The Velvet Underground Story*: Courtesy of Cooper Square Press. Marc Jacobs sunglasses.
PAGE 16: Ronnie Spector: Courtesy of Retna. *The Best of the Ronettes*: Courtesy of EMI. Jacket Cover, copyright 1990 by Random House, Inc., from *Be My Baby* by Ronnie Spector and Vince Waldron. Used by permission of Harmony Books, a division of Random House, Inc.
PAGE 17: The Ronettes: Courtesy of Everett Collection. Hair Do 22" Clip-In Extensions in Midnight Brown. Cover Girl Line Exact Liquid Liner Pen in Very Black.
PAGE 18: Francoise Hardy: Courtesy of Everett Collection. Leather Jacket by G-Star. *Comment Te Dire Adieu*: Courtesy of Francoise Hardy.
PAGE 19: Dusty Springfield: Courtesy of Everett Collection. *Dusty in Memphis*: Courtesy of Universal Music Enterprises. M.A.C Matte Black Eyeshadow.
PAGE 20: Jane Birkin: Courtesy of Everett Collection. *Blow-Up*: Courtesy of Bridge Films.
PAGE 21: Jane Birkin and Serge Gainsbourg: Courtesy of Everett Collection. Miller Harris L'Air de Rien. *Histoire de Melody Nelson*: Courtesy of Universal Music Enterprises. *Jane Birkin et Serge Gainsbourg*: Courtesy of Universal Music Enterprises.
PAGE 22: Nancy Sinatra: Courtesy of Everett Collection.
PAGE 23: *Movin' With Nancy*, *Boots*, and *Nancy Sinatra*: all, courtesy of Boots Enterprises/nancysinatra.com. Vintage boots from Screaming Mimi's. Shu Uemura False Eyelashes 600.
PAGE 24: Tina Turner: Courtesy of Retna. *Proud Mary: The Best of Ike and Tina Turner*: Courtesy of EMI. *Mad Max Beyond Thunderdome*: Courtesy Kennedy Miller Productions. Stilettos by Christian Louboutin.
PAGE 25: Janis Joplin: Courtesy of Everett Collection. Jeans by Dittos. *Pearl*: Courtesy of SonyBMG Music Entertainment.
PAGE 26: Suzi Quatro: Courtesy of Everett Collection. Status Graphite Stealth bass: courtesy of Status Graphite. *Can the Can*: Courtesy of Suzi Quatro. Photograph by Gered Mankowitz.
PAGE 27: Betty Davis: Courtesy of Light in the Attic Records. Antonio's Styling Pik. Platform boots by Robert Clergerie. *Betty Davis*: Courtesy of Light in the Attic Records.
PAGE 28: The Slits: Courtesy of Everett Collection. *Cut*: Courtesy of Island Records.
PAGE 29: The Slits: Courtesy of Everett Collection. *England's Dreaming*: Courtesy of Jon Savage. Skirt by Dollhouse.
PAGE 30: The Runaways: Courtesy of Retna. Boot by Giuseppe Zanotti. Gold leggings by American Apparel. *Foxes*: Courtesy Casablanca Film Works.
PAGE 31: B.C. Rich Mockingbird guitar, bcrich.com. *The Runaways*: Courtesy of Cherry Red Records. *I Love Rock 'n' Roll*: Courtesy of Blackheart Records Group; photograph by Mick Rock.

PAGE 32: Chrissie Hynde: Courtesy of Retna. *The Pretenders*: Courtesy of Warner Brothers. Levi's vest, vintage.
PAGE 33: Patti Smith: Courtesy of Everett Collection. *Please Kill Me*: Courtesy of Penguin. *Horses*: Courtesy of SonyBMG Music Entertainment.
PAGE 34: Debbie Harry: Courtesy of Retna.
PAGE 35: *Eat to the Beat*: Courtesy of EMI. *Parallel Lines*: Courtesy of EMI. *Making Tracks: The Rise of Blondie*: Courtesy of the Perseus Books Group.
PAGE 36: Tina Weymouth: Courtesy of Retna. *Talking Heads 77*: Courtesy of Warner Brothers. *Tom Tom Club*: Courtesy of Warner Brothers.
PAGE 37: Poly Styrene: Courtesy of Retna. *Germ Free Adolescents*: Courtesy of EMI. *Punk Attitude*: Courtesy of 3DD Productions.
PAGE 38: Kate Bush: Courtesy of Retna. Leotard by American Apparel. *Wuthering Heights*: Courtesy of Barnes & Noble. *Hounds of Love*: Courtesy of EMI UK.
PAGE 39: Siouxsie Sioux: Courtesy of Everett Collection. Bra by Alexander Wang.Stila Smudge Pot in Black. *Kaleidoscope*: Courtesy of Universal Music Enterprises.
PAGE 40: Olivia Newton-John: Courtesy of Everett Collection. *If You Love Me, Let Me Know*: Courtesy of Universal Music Enterprises. *Physical*: Courtesy of Universal Music Enterprises. *Xanadu*: Courtesy of Universal Pictures. Rimmel Soft Kohl Kajal Eye Pencil in Cool Blue.
PAGE 41: The Go-Go's: Courtesy of Retna. Earrings by GirlPROPS. *Beauty and the Beat*: Courtesy of EMI.
PAGE 42: Stevie Nicks: Courtesy of Retna.
PAGE 43: *Rumours*: Courtesy of Warner Brothers. *Bella Donna*: Courtesy of Warner Brothers. Hat by 3.1 Phillip Lim with feather by American Plume & Fancy Feather Company. Boots by Renton Western Wear, available on amazon.com.
PAGE 44: Pat Benatar: Courtesy of Everett Collection. Shiseido Accentuating Color Stick in Rosy Flush. Boot by Belle by Sigerson Morrison. *In the Heat of the Night*: Courtesy of EMI.
PAGE 45: Heart: Courtesy of Retna. HD-35 Nancy Wilson Signature Edition Acoustic Guitar by C.F. Martin & Co. *Dreamboat Annie*: Courtesy of Warner Brothers. *Little Queen*: Courtesy of SonyBMG Music Entertainment.
PAGE 46: Tanya Donelly: Courtesy of Retna. *The Real Ramona*: Courtesy of 4AD; Graphic Design by V23 for 4AD. *Pod*: Courtesy of 4AD; Graphic Design by V23 for 4AD. *Star*: Courtesy of Warner Brothers.
PAGE 47: Kim Deal: Courtesy of Retna. Bumble and Bumble Brown Hair Powder. *Doolittle*: Courtesy of 4AD; Graphic Design by V23 for 4AD. *Last Splash*: Courtesy of 4AD; Graphic Design by V23 for 4AD.
PAGE 48: Kim Gordon: photographed by Stefano Giovannini. *The Year Punk Broke*: Courtesy of Tara Films.
PAGE 49: *Daydream Nation*: Courtesy of Universal. *Goo*: Courtesy of Universal. Skirt by Lux at Urban Outfitters. Guitar strap by Built by Wendy.
PAGE 50: Liz Phair: Courtesy of Retna. Urban Decay Eye Shadow in Polyester Bride. Little black book by Graphic Image, Inc. *Exile in Guyville*: Courtesy of Matador Records.
PAGE 51: Le Tigre: Courtesy of of Girlie Action PR. *Le Tigre*: Courtesy of Le Tigre. *Bikini Kill*: Courtesy of Mr. Lady Records. *The Feminine Mystique*: Courtesy of Penguin Books.
PAGE 52: Courtney Love: Courtesy of Everett Collection. *Live Through This*: Courtesy of Universal. *Celebrity Skin*: Courtesy of Universal Music Enterprises. Revlon Super Lustrous Lipstick in Fire & Ice. *Sid & Nancy*: The Samuel Goldwyn Company.
PAGE 53: Courtney Love: Courtesy of Everett Collection. Goody StayPut Barrettes. *Dirty Blonde*: Courtesy of Farrar, Straus & Giroux.
PAGE 54: Kylie Minogue: Courtesy of Everett Collection.
PAGE 55: Kylie Minogue and Michael Hutchence: Courtesy of Everett Collection. Murad Firm and Tone Serum. Hot

Pants by D&G. *Fever*: Courtesy of EMI UK.

PAGE 56: Bjork: photographed by Terry Richardson.

PAGE 57: Bjork: photographed by Terry Richardson. Make Up For Ever Twelve Grease Paint Case. *Debut*: Courtesy of Warner Brothers. *Homogenic*: Courtesy of Warner Brothers.

PAGE 58: Fiona Apple: photographed by Jason Nocito. TIGI Bed Head Mastermind Hair Candy. *Extraordinary Machine*: Courtesy of SonyBMG Music Entertainment. *Tidal*: Courtesy of SonyBMG Music Entertainment.

PAGE 59: Justine Frischmann: Courtesy of Everett Collection. Boots by Doc Martens. *The Menace*: Courtesy of Warner Brothers. *Elastica*: Courtesy of Universal.

PAGE 60: Missy Elliott: Courtesy of Retna. adidas Original Respect M.E. sneakers by Missy Elliott. M.A.C Lipglass in Oh Baby. *Under Construction*: Courtesy of Warner Brothers.

PAGE 61: Lady Sovereign: photographed by Alexander Thompson. Tracksuit jacket by adidas Originals. *Public Warning*: Courtesy of Island/Def Jam.

PAGE 62: Cat Power: photographed by Stefano Giovannini. M.A.C Eye Pencil in Ebony.

PAGE 63: Cat Power: Courtesy of Retna. Nashville Telecaster Deluxe guitar by Fender. *The Covers Record*: Courtesy of Matador Records. *The Greatest*: Courtesy of Matador Records.

PAGE 64: PJ Harvey: Courtesy of Everett Collection. Gold dress by H & M.

PAGE 65: PJ Harvey: photographed by Valeria Phillips. *Rid of Me*: Courtesy of Island Records. *Stories from the City, Stories from the Sea*: Courtesy of Island Records. *White Chalk*: Courtesy of Island Records.

PAGE 66: The White Stripes: photographed by Kenneth Capello. *Elephant*: Courtesy of The White Stripes. *Get Behind Me Satan*: Courtesy of The White Stripes. *Under Blackpool Lights*: Courtesy of The White Stripes.

PAGE 67: Alison Mosshart: Courtesy of Everett Collection. *No Wow*: Courtesy of Rough Trade. Jeans by Levi's.

PAGE 68: Karen O: Courtesy of Everett Collection. NARS lipstick in Jungle Red.

PAGE 69: Karen O: Courtesy of Retna. *Fever to Tell*: Courtesy of Universal Music Enterprises. *Yeah Yeah Yeahs*: Courtesy of Wichita Recordings. *Is Is*: Courtesy of Universal Music Enterprises. Fingerless gloves by LaCrasia.

PAGE 70: Joanna Newsom: photographed by Bryan Rindfuss. Fur hat by Eugenia Kim. *Roget's College Thesaurus. Ys*: Courtesy of Drag City.

PAGE 71: Lily Allen: photographed by JAM. *Alright, Still*: 2007 EMI Records under exclusive license to Capitol Records, Inc. Lily Allen appears courtesy of Capitol Records, Inc. Earrings by GirlPROPS.

PAGE 72: M.I.A: Courtesy of Retna. *Kala*: Courtesy of Interscope. *Arular*: Courtesy of Interscope.

PAGE 73: M.I.A.: photographed by Matt Irwin. Creative Nail Design in Hot Pop Yellow, available at cnd.com; Mattese NYC in Parrot Green, available at Ricky's. Leggings by Danskin (see danskin.com).

PAGE 74: Amy Winehouse: photographed by Mari Sarai. L'Oréal Paris Voluminous Mistake-Proof Marker in Black. Lush Rehab Shampoo. *Back to Black*: Courtesy of Universal Music Enterprises.

PAGE 75: Beth Ditto: photographed by Danielle St. Laurent. *Standing in the Way of Control*: Courtesy of Kill Rock Stars. Dress by Betsey Johnson.

PAGE 78: The Donnas: photographed by Marvin Scott Jarrett. *Highway to Hell*: Courtesy of Warner Brothers. *Dirty*: Courtesy of Universal Music Enterprises. *Mirror Moves*: Courtesy of SonyBMG. *ABBA Gold*: Courtesy of Universal Music Enterprises. *Too Fast for Love*: Courtesy of Beyond Records.

PAGE 79: Britney Spears: Courtesy of Everett Collection; Ratt: Courtesy of Retna; Wendy O. Williams: Courtesy of Retna.

PAGE 80: New Young Pony Club: Courtesy of Modular People. *Fun House*: Courtesy of Warner Brothers. *Fear of a Black Planet*: Courtesy of Island/Def Jam. *Dummy*: Courtesy of Universal Music Enterprises.

PAGE 81: Ava Gardner: Courtesy of Retna; Bettie Page: Courtesy of Everett Collection; Iggy Pop: Courtesy of Retna ; Rita Hayworth: Courtesy of Everett Collection. The Scissor Sisters photographed by Alexander Thompson.

PAGE 82: Jenny Lewis: photographed by Patrick O'Dell; The Carpenters: Courtesy of Retna; Pavement: Courtesy of Retna

PAGE 83: *Transformer*: Courtesy of SonyBMG Music Entertainment. *There's Nothing Wrong with Love*: Courtesy of Built to Spill. *Crooked Rain, Crooked Rain*: Courtesy of Matador Records. *Gonna Take a Miracle*: Courtesy of SonyBMG Music Entertainment. *Three Feet High and Rising*: Courtesy of Tommy Boy Records.

PAGE 84: Plasticines: photographed by Pejman Birounvand; The B-52's: Courtesy of Retna. *Blondie*: Courtesy of EMI. *24 Hour Party People*: Courtesy of MGM Studios. *Because of the Times*: Courtesy of SonyBMG Music Entertainment.

PAGE 85: Plasticines: photographed by Pejman Birounvand; Debbie Harry with Blondie: Courtesy of Retna; Patti Smith: Courtesy of Everett Collection; The Ramones: Courtesy of Retna.

PAGE 86: Juliette Lewis: photographed by Stacey Mark

PAGE 87: David Lee Roth: Courtesy of Retna; *Rocky Horror Picture Show*: Courtesy of Everett Collection; Nina Simone: Courtesy of Everett Collection; The Jimi Hendrix Experience: Courtesy of Everett Collection

PAGE 88: Eleanor Friedberger: photographed by Stacey Mark. *The Sound of Music*: Courtesy of 20th Century Fox. *Physical Graffiti*: Courtesy of Warner Brothers. *Astral Weeks*: Courtesy of Warner Brothers. *Ethiopiques, Vol 3*: Courtesy of Buda Musique.

PAGE 89: Ronnie Lane: Courtesy of Everett Collection; Woody Allen: Courtesy of Everett Collection; Donald Sutherland: Courtesy of Everett Collection.

PAGE 90: Keren Ann: photographed by Joshua Wildman; *The Ghost of Tom Joad*: Courtesy of SonyBMG Music Entertainment. Mamas and the Papas Greatest Hits: Courtesy of Universal Music Enterprises. *Let's Get Lost*: Courtesy of Novus.

PAGE 91: Jane Birkin and Serge Gainsbourg Courtesy of Everett. Billie Holiday: Courtesy of Everett Collection. John Lennon: Courtesy of Everett Collection. Alfred Hitchcock: Courtesy of Everett Collection. Bob Marley: Courtesy of Retna. *This is Spinal Tap*: Courtesy of MGM Studios.

PAGE 92: Tegan and Sara: photographed by Abbey Drucker. *Siamese Dream*: Courtesy of EMI. *Born in the USA*: Courtesy of SonyBMG Music Entertainment.

PAGE 93: Sting and the Police: Courtesy of Retna; Bruce Springsteen: Courtesy of Retna; Elton John: Courtesy of Retna.

PAGE 94: Luiza Sá: photographed by Esther Varella. *Sonic Youth; Corporate Ghost*: Courtesy of Universal Music Enterprises. *Rid of Me*: Courtesy of Island Records. *Is This It?*: Courtesy of SonyBMG. *The Velvet Underground & Nico*: Courtesy of Universal Music Enterprises. *No Direction Home*: Courtesy of Paramount Pictures.

PAGE 95: Chloë Sevigny: Courtesy of Retna. Madonna: Courtesy of Everett Collection. Traci Lords: Courtesy of Everett Collection.

PAGE 96: The Long Blondes: photographed by Borden Capalino. *Cowboy in Sweden*: Courtesy of Smells Like Records/Lee Hazlewood. *Appetite for Destruction*: Courtesy of Universal Music Enterprises. *Le Tigre*: Courtesey of Le Tigre.

PAGE 97: Sherilyn Fenn: Courtesy of Everett Collection. ABBA: Courtesy of Retna. Faye Dunaway: Courtesy of Retna.

PAGE 98: Bat for Lashes: photographed by Todd Selby. *Thriller*: Courtesy of SonyBMG Music Entertainment. *The Essential Heart*: Courtesy of SonyBMG Music Entertainment. *Disintegration*: Courtesy of Warner Brothers. *Fleetwood Mac*: Courtesy of Warner Brothers.

PAGE 99: Elizabeth Taylor: Courtesy of Retna. Patricia Arquette: Courtesy of Everett Collection. Judy Garland: Courtesy of Everett Collection.

PAGE 100: Peaches: photographed by Kenneth Cappello; Grace Jones: Courtesy of Retna.

PAGE 101: Girlschool: Courtesy of Everett Collection.

Prince: Courtesy of Retna. *Trans-Europe Express*: Courtesy of EMI. *The Stooges*: Courtesy of Warner Brothers. *To Bring You My Love*: Courtesy of Island Records. *Bad Girls*: Courtesy of Island Records. *Hot, Cool and Vicious*: Courtesy of Universal Music Enterprises.

PAGE 102: Justine D: photographed by Alexander Thompson. *Blue Train*: Courtesy of EMI. *The Sky's Gone Out*: Courtesy of Universal Music Enterprises.

PAGE 103: Helmut Newton photograph: Courtesy of Retna; Diane Keaton. Courtesy of Everett Collection. *Biba*: Courtesy of Retna. David Bowie: Courtesy of Retna.

PAGE 104: The MisShapes: photographed by Vorrasi.

PAGE 105: Jarvis Cocker: Courtesy of Retna. Siouxsie Sioux: Courtesy of Everett Collection. John Lennon and Yoko Ono: Courtesy of Everett Collection.

PAGE 106: Sharin Foo: photographed by Emma Summerton. *Bringing It All Back Home*: Courtesy of SonyBMG Music Entertainment. *Scott 3*: Courtesy of UME Imports. *Laughing Stock*: Courtesy of Universal Music Enterprises. *Harvest*: Courtesy of Warner Brothers.

PAGE 107: Monica Vitti: Courtesy of Retna. Marlene Dietrich: Courtesy of Retna. Joni Mitchell: Courtesy of Retna.

PAGE 110: Kate Nash: photographed by Jason Frank Rothenberg.

PAGE 111: *Moldy Peaches*: Courtesy of SonyBMG. *Pussy Whipped*: Courtesy of Mr. Lady Records. *Post*: Courtesy of Warner Brothers. *Singles Going Steady*: Courtesy of EMI. *Room on Fire*: Courtesy of SonyBMG.

PAGE 112: Eisley: photographed by Bryan Rindfuss.

PAGE 113: *Speak for Yourself*: Courtesy of SonyBMG Music Entertainment. *Transfiguration of Vincent*: Courtesy of Merge. *Good News For People Who Love Bad News*: Courtesy of SonyBMG Music Entertainment. *Tapestry*: Courtesy of SonyBMG Music Entertainment. *Rumours*: Courtesy of Warner Brothers. *In the Aeroplane Over the Sea*: Courtesy of Merge. *Abbey Road*: Courtesy of EMI. *Coming Home*: Courtesy of Universal Music Enterprises.

PAGE 114: The Like: photographed by Marvin Scott Jarrett.

PAGE 115: *Nilsson Schmilsson*: Courtesy of SonyBMG Music Entertainment. *Rum Sodomy & the Lash*: Courtesy of Warner Brothers. *Heart Food*: Courtesy of Warner Brothers. *Royal Trux*: Courtesy of Drag City.

PAGE 116: The Watson Twins: photographed by Jesse Dylan.

PAGE 117: *Bringing it All Back Home*: Courtesy of SonyBMG. *Woman to Woman*: Courtesy of Stax Records/ Concord Music Group. *Honeysuckle Rose*: Courtesy of SonyBMG Music Entertainment. *Déjà Vu*: Courtesy of Warner Brothers. *Bookends*: Courtesy of SonyBMG Music Entertainment. *Different Light*: Courtesy of SonyBMG Music Entertainment.

PAGE 118: Au Revoir Simone: photographed by Borden Capalino.

PAGE 119: *The Golden Vessyl of Sound*: Courtesy of K Records. *Exile in Guyville*: Courtesy of Matador Records. *Sweden*: Courtesy of Shrimper Records. *Imagine*: Yoko Ono Lennon, courtesy of Yoko Ono. *Saturday Night Fever Soundtrack*: Courtesy of Universal Music Enterprises. *Dandelion Gum*: Cover by Tabacco.

PAGE 120: The Handsome Furs: photographed by Joseph Yarmush.

PAGE 121: *Exuma II*: Courtesy of Repertoire Records. *Chairs Missing*: Courtesy of Warner Brothers. *The Nerves EP*: Thanks to the Nerves. *Revolutionary Vol. 2*: Painting by Anton Fletcher. *Easter*: Courtesy of SonyBMG Music Entertainment. *Jolene*: Courtesy of SonyBMG Music Entertainment. *Surfin on Heroin*: Courtesy of Warner Brothers.

PAGE 122: Thurston Moore: photographed by Isabel Asha Penzilen.

PAGE 123: *The Monkees Greatest Hits*: Courtesy of Warner Brothers. *Get Together the Essential Youngbloods*: Courtesy of SonyBMG Music Entertainment. *Ramones*: Courtesy of Warner Brothers. *Patti Smith: The Patti Smith Masters*: Courtesy of SonyBMG Music Entertainment. *Nirvana Singles Box Set*: Courtesy of Universal Music Enterprises.

PAGE 124: The Go! Team: photographed by Erin Barry.

PAGE 125: *Songs From a Room*: Courtesy of SonyBMG Music Entertainment. *Ill Communication*: Courtesy of Grand Royal Records. *Alice*: Courtesy of Anti. *Sister*: Courtesy of Universal Music Enterprises. *Myrmidons of*

Melodrama: Courtesy of Cherry Red Records. *I See a Darkness*: Courtesy of Palace Records.

PAGE 126: Charlotte Cooper: photographed by Justin Hollar.

PAGE 127: *Franz Ferdinand*: Courtesy of Domino Records. *Loose*: Courtesy of Universal Music Enterprises. *Cansei de Ser Sexy*: Courtesy of Sub Pop Records. *Louder Now*: Courtesy of Warner Brothers. *Absolution*: Courtesy of Warner Brothers. *Bleach*: Courtesy of Sub Pop Records. *The Milk-Eyed Mender*: Courtesy of Drag City.

PAGE 128: Samantha Ronson: Courtesy of Courtesy of Everett Collection.

PAGE 129: *For Once in My Life*: Courtesy of Universal Music Enterprises. *Blind Faith*: Courtesy of Universal Music Enterprises. *Foreigner*: Courtesy of Warner Brothers. *Blue*: Courtesy of Warner Brothers. *Axis: Bold as Love*: Courtesy of Universal Music Enterprises. *I Wish It Would Rain*: Courtesy of Universal Music Enterprises. *The End of Innocence*: Courtesy of Universal Music Enterprises. *Revolver*: Courtesy of EMI.

PAGE 130: Sarah Lewitinn: photographed by Reynard Li.

PAGE 131: *Porcupine*: Courtesy of Warner Brothers. *Funeral*: Courtesy of Merge. *Placebo*: Photo by Saul Fletcher; design by Blue Source. *Best Stop Pop*: Courtesy of Stolen Transmission; design by the Oohlas and Greg Jacobson, photography by Dan Bush. *Antics*: Courtesy of Matador Records. *Louder than Bombs*: Courtesy of Warner Brothers. *Hot Fuss*: Courtesy of Island Records. *Live Through This*: Courtesy of Universal.

PAGE 134: The Flaming Lips: Photographed by Michelle Martin-Coyne

PAGE 136: The Horrors: photographed by Roberta Ridolfi

PAGE 138: The Grates: photographed by Patrick Fraser

PAGE 140: Maya Wilde: Courtesy of Maya Wilde.

PAGE 142: Steve Aoki: photographed by Ruvan Wijesooriya

PAGE 144: Mooka Kinney: photographed by Alexandra Gershman

PAGE 146: Art Brut: photographed by Michael Nevin

PAGE 148: JD Samson: Photographed by Cass Bird.

FRONT & BACK COVER:

Plasticines photographed by Marvin Scott Jarret

Every effort has been made by *NYLON* magazine to identify and contact the copyright holder for all images in this book, including photographs, album covers, and book covers. Any inaccuracies brought to our attention will be corrected for future editions.

ACKNOWLEDGMENTS

On behalf of NYLON, April Long
would like to thank:

Marvin Scott Jarrett
Jaclynn Jarrett
Winona Barton-Ballentine
Stephen Walker
Carl Williamson
Caitlin Leffel
Charles Miers
Ellen Nidy
Allison Power
Elizabeth Smith
Michele Outland
Josh Gurrie
Nicole Michalek
Fiorella Valdesolo
Charlotte Rudge
Nikki Schneider
Kate Williams
Luke Crisell
Andie Cusick
Samantha Gilewicz
Lina Plioplyte
Ceasar Vega
Vanessa Hudson
John Espinosa
Janenc Otten
Glenn Bradie
Caroline Sturgess
Alison Jo Rigney
The Everett Collection
Retna
Bidceps
Chinae Alexander
Danielle Prescod
Tina Riopel
Michelle Reneau
Aubrey Stallard
Jessica Williamson

This edition first published in 2008
by UNIVERSE PUBLISHING
A Division of
Rizzoli International Publications, Inc.
300 Park Avenue South
New York NY 10010
www.rizzoliusa.com

Design by Circle & Square
Text by April Long
Edited by Caitlin Leffel

2008 2009 2010 2011
10 9 8 7 6 5 4 3 2 1
First Edition

Printed in China

ISBN-13:
978-0-7893-1692-9
Library of Congress Control Number:
2007939896